HOW NOT TO KILL YOURSELF

A Survival Guide for Imaginative Pessimists

SET SYTES
& FAITH G. HARPER, PHD

Microcosm Publishing
Portland, OR

HOW NOT TO KILL YOURSELF
A Survival Guide for Imaginative Pessimists

Part of the 5 Minute Therapy Series

© Set Sytes, 2014, 2016, 2018
This edition © Microcosm Publishing, 2018
First edition, first published 2016
Third edition, first published March 14, 2018

ISBN 978-1-62106-197-7
This is Microcosm #267
Cover and book design by Joe Biel
Distributed by PGW and Turnaround in the UK

For a catalog, write or visit:
Microcosm Publishing
2752 N Williams Ave.
Portland, OR 97227
(503)799-2698
MicrocosmPublishing.com

If you bought this on Amazon, I'm so sorry because you could have gotten it cheaper and supported a small, independent publisher at MicrocosmPublishing. com

Global labor conditions are bad, and our roots in industrial Cleveland in the 70s and 80s made us appreciate the need to treat workers right. Therefore, our books are MADE IN THE USA and printed on post-consumer paper.

Library of Congress Cataloging-in-Publication Data

Names: Sytes, Set, author.
Title: How not to kill yourself : a survival guide for imaginative pessimists
    / Set Sytes.
Description: Third Edition. | Portland, OR : Microcosm Publishing, [2017] |
    Revised edition of the author's How not to kill yourself, 2016.
Identifiers: LCCN 2017014401 (print) | LCCN 2017017853 (ebook) | ISBN
    9781621065807 (ebook) | ISBN 9781621061977 (pbk.)
Subjects: LCSH: Self-actualization (Psychology) | Depression, Mental. |
    Suicide--Prevention. | Zines.
Classification: LCC BF637.S4 (ebook) | LCC BF637.S4 S978 2017 (print) | DDC
    155.2--dc23
LC record available at https://lccn.loc.gov/2017014401

MICROCOSM · PUBLISHING

Microcosm Publishing is Portland's most diversified publishing house and distributor with a focus on the colorful, authentic, and empowering. Our books and zines have put your power in your hands since 1996, equipping readers to make positive changes in their lives and in the world around them. Microcosm emphasizes skill-building, showing hidden histories, and fostering creativity through challenging conventional publishing wisdom with books and bookettes about DIY skills, food, bicycling, gender, self-care, and social justice. What was once a distro and record label was started by Joe Biel in his bedroom and has become among the oldest independent publishing houses in Portland, OR. We are a politically moderate, centrist publisher in a world that has inched to the right for the past 80 years.

CONTENTS

FOREWORD
BY FAITH G. HARPER PHD

You have this book in your hands due to the wonderment that is the life force of the universe.

Which, in this instance, worked its magic through Amazon algorithms. Because CLEARLY life force energy isn't picky about how it gets the job done.

Amazon suggested that I buy this ebook by some dude named Set Sytes called *How Not to Kill Yourself*. It was only a couple of bucks and I spend at least that much on coffee every day, so I thought *sure, why not.*

And holy shitballs, this little book was brilliant. I had a tech-savvy friend strip it to a PDF so I could print it to have sitting in my waiting room so I could show people how great it is and why, they too needed to spend $1.99 to download it.

(That, by the way, is totally illegal. And in violation of Amazon policies. And generally uncool. So don't ever do that, OK? I did it

for the greater good and it totally worked out well. But seriously, don't try that at home. It's bad juju. Ahem. Moving on.)

So I'm a therapist. It was in my office. It was well loved. To the point that my printed copy, in a pretty binder with a note on the cover encouraging waiting room peeps to go purchase their own copy, disappeared pretty quickly.

Things don't generally disappear from my waiting room, so I figured whoever took it was really needing it.

I sent my PDF copy to Microcosm Publishing. They're my publisher and pretty fucking cool about publishing the things the world really is looking to read that no one else has the balls to publish.

And I told them: "Y'all need to find this guy and publish this shit. If only so I can order multiple copies to give out in my waiting room since I can't get people to download their own legit copy and it keeps disappearing."

And they read it and said "Oh, FUCK YEAH, we're down."

And they tracked down Set Sytes. Who thought we were all batshit crazy (which is not at all an irrational response to an email from people you don't know in a country you don't even live in).

Eventually he realized that everyone involved *was* crazy, but in a kinda good way. And he agreed to let Microcosm convert his ebook into a zine.

This zine did great, y'all. Cuz it *is* great. So, within about three minutes, Microcosm asked Set to expand it into a book. So he did that, too.

Then they asked me to write the intro. So I could confess my illegal book hacking shenanigans that all worked out in the end because Set got a book contract. Or rather, because my illegal book hacking shenanigans led to a book that is helping to save lives. It's a book that people pick up and read out loud to each other at the bookstore. That makes people teary-eyed and giggly at the same time. It's a book that helps. It's a book that works.

If you haven't yet been made aware of the magic of this little book, you may now be asking: *What's one more fucking book about suicidality going to do?* You've been through this, right? Either for yourself or with a loved one. Because no one picks up books about suicidality if it isn't affecting their life in some kinda fucked-up way. And nothing has really helped. Not entirely. Suicidality is still always there, lurking in the corners. Shit-talking you right outside your consciousness. Finishing off the tub of ice cream in the freezer. Leaving the fuel tank on empty and a dent on the bumper. Nut-punching you just when you thought maybe you had space to breathe again.

Suicidality is an EPIC FUCKING ASSHOLE. And you are wondering to yourself, why am I trying *one more book?*

You're trying one more book because Set totally gets it. He knows and he agrees. And he figured out something really fucking valuable in all this mess. How to stay alive *anyway*. Not barely, not begrudgingly. Not in a sorta-kinda at least for now but we will see about next week kind of way. Not to shut up some stupid therapist like me and to keep himself from getting hospitalized by them.

He figured out something real and true, in that deep-down place you are searching for within your own life.

Staying alive with a brain bent on self-annihilation, in a world that doesn't necessarily value your worth, is the ultimate radical act.

This world has taken too much from you. From all of us. *And it doesn't get to take anymore.* It doesn't get to crush our spirit, define our worth, or police our existence. We are here because we are supposed to be. Because we have shit to figure out along the way. And there is value in the struggle. Which means there is value in all of us, all the time, for any and all of the reasons we choose.

Because sometimes that is all we can do.

Continue to breathe in and out. Continuing to be here despite everything *is resistance in its own right*. Knowing that you are out there, reading this book and fighting for yourself is what makes this all bearable *for me*. And I'm selfish like that. I love knowing you (and Set, and the amazing people at Microcosm Publishing, and all us other weirdos and misfits and rebel alliance folks) are here with me being radically, subversively alive. So, thank you for that. Seriously. Thank you for being here. We got this.

—Faith G. Harper, PhD, LPC-S, ACS, ACN

www.theintimacydr.com

A STARRY-EYED PREAMBLE

"I know it's crooked, but it's the only game in town."

–Canada Bill Jones

I'm here to save your life.

Well, not really. I don't have nearly enough traveling money to get to you all. But I *am* here to help you save your own life. You're already fighting your fight. I'm just here to give you a triple-barreled shotgun to fight it with. Or a cat that shoots fireballs. Take your pick.

I'm not here to tell you that the world is actually fabulous, and you'll just have to damn well learn to appreciate it. That the world is beautiful and full of, I don't know, kittens and rainbow-sprouting unicorns. That you'll see all this amazingness as soon as a passing wizard gives you some new eyes (and a new brain).

Sure, there might be some nice things in the world. I guess. But there's also a lot of ugliness. And, even worse than that, is all the mundanity. I'd hazard the world is comprised of about 99% boring, lifeless, drab, meaningless, empty whatever.

So, no, the world won't be your savior. And chances are, unless you've just taken a lot of psychedelics, you won't roll over one day with stars in your *kawaii* eyes, curling into a trembling ball of joy as kittens dance in the clouds and infinite lances of sunlight daub the world gold.

The answer to getting better, and to not killing yourself, isn't in the kittens and puppies, it isn't in the clouds, it isn't in the orangutans in the rainforests or the fireworks in the night sky.

The core reason, the truest, most sincere reason to stay alive isn't really out there at all.

It's in you.

You are the key and you are the lock. You are the whole meaningful universe. And I promise you that's not just me being hippie. This isn't a spiritual guide. There are no chakras here, no healing auras or "positive energies." I have a real, practical point to make.

It's a terribly sad state of affairs, but as long as you stay mute and withdrawn, the world just won't care about you. That's because it doesn't know you.

I think it's about time to change that.

POINTLESS CAVEAT

There are all sorts of reasons people have to kill themselves, because there are all sorts of people. I could not hope to tackle all this, and I would be severely out of my depth if I tried.

I assume, however, that you were drawn to two things. The title, which perhaps suggested something black-humored, something partly tongue-in-cheek, to you. And the subtitle, that targets you specifically (if I've got the wrong person, then this book might not be for you, but by all means give it a jolly good go).

So: all sorts of reasons, all sorts of people. This is directed at a certain type of person—a lump category I have called "imaginative pessimists." I could have also called them (and me) "creative cynics," or the classic and much maligned "tortured artists." Or maybe just "weirdos" (I mean that in the nicest way—the best people are at least a little weird). This guide is attempting to cater to your particular sense of self, and I want you to be proud of that self.

I appreciate that a number of the things I say will fall flat to you. After all, you're a gigantic group of individuals. Every one of you is unique. If I *did* somehow magic you all into an actual physical group together, within ten minutes two-thirds of you would have wandered off out of sight and the other third would be sitting on the floor determinedly avoiding eye contact. I'd be insane to think I could assume you're all the same. I just hope that you'll all get something out of reading this.

And, let me just get this out of the way: you've done a fucking good job getting this far. Well done you. I really mean that.

WHO THE HELL ARE YOU?

Tell me if any of this is true (I don't know how you'd tell me, just pretend. You're good at that):

- You prefer dreams to real, waking life.

- You prefer fiction and fantasy to the outside world.

- You would like to live inside your own head (the good parts of it, I mean, not the depressing parts).

- You're often "in your own little world" or "away with the fairies" or whatever other rubbish people say.

- It is the world that gets you down, and all it demands of you. You frequently find the world—or simply humanity—quite awful. It is drab, boring, mundane, and depressing. It might even be cruel. It is certainly nothing like how you want it to be.

- The only things that could be considered wrong with you could also be considered the fault of the world around you. There is little-to-nothing intrinsically wrong with you (if you don't believe this, that's fine—but at least consider it).

- You make heavy use of escapism (e.g. books, movies, games, television, flights of fancy).

- You are highly creative and imaginative.

- Sometimes you feel like you have a bit of an ego, or a spot of narcissism.

- You are sensitive, and easily wound up by things/people. Especially when you spend a long time overthinking things.

- You long for new things, while at the same time longing for innocence.

- You don't get as much pleasure out of the same things as you used to. You wish you could see the world and the things in it as you used to, or as other, happier people seem to.

- You have a strong, and yet sometimes unusual, sense of humor.

- People making such a big division in life between childhood and adulthood annoys and depresses you, and you hate being told to "grow up" or that being "childish" is a bad thing.

● You wish sometimes that you were not so cynical, but part of you also feels superior for your cynicism, that you are "in the right."

And so on, you get the idea.

If you are tutting and shaking your head at some of these, this survival guide might not be for you.

A NOT-SO-DELICATE WARNING

In this guide, there will be swear words. I think I've already used one. I do not tip-toe around heavy topics. Suicide is a monster of a thing, a creature that deserves to be, at turns, fought with poisoned swords and poisoned words, shouted down and sworn at, laughed at and, above all, listened to. If you are offended by swear words in this context, perhaps you should re-examine your priorities, or read a more PC book.

Suicide is not PC, and it never will be. It does not give a fuck.

This guide will be, at turns, aggressive, tongue-in-cheek, sympathetic, empathetic, and maybe even fawning. The latter is because, if people really knew and understood everything, completely knew and understood each other, completely knew and understood *you*, and yet also looked at and thought about everything as though they were seeing it and hearing it and thinking it for the very first time, you'd be worshipped.

We'll get to this absurd suggestion eventually. For now, accept that it is both my duty and yours to stroke your own ego.

THE CAUSE

In this guide, there will be many assumptions made. I am not about to litter every sentence with a caveat, or prefix every paragraph with a "if this isn't you, skip a bit." Every person is different, and every imaginative pessimist is different. Reasons for suicide are all different. And sure, I'll be wrong about you. I don't know you. I'm hoping, if you're reasonably satisfied with the label "imaginative pessimist," you'll want to keep reading without wanting to throw me in a river. Besides, good luck catching me! I can run like the devil when I need to.

Many reasons. But this isn't about your partner leaving you, about losing someone close to you, about losing your job, about bad family and worse friends, about dead-end work (or no work at all) and drug habits and, basically, life punching you in the face one too many times over.

Here's my first big assumption. These things may have pushed you right to the edge, but they weren't the *core* reasons. Life gives us hard knocks, and sometimes they can take our teeth. Most people get back up. Some don't want to, but still do. Some don't want to, and don't.

You're not mad, and there's nothing wrong with you (well, in this context, at least!). If you take anti-depressants or whatever other medication, go on taking it, if it's proven to help long-term. Listen to your doctor; get a second (doctor's!) opinion if needed. Find a therapist or psychiatrist, and then find another as soon as you realize you don't like them. Get all the professional help and support you can get. Mental illness and similar things are not the focus of this guide. I am not a doctor.

I'm going to tackle this from the widest angle I can:

You want to die because of who you are, and what the world is.

This is no temporary thing. This is no flash in the pan. You have lived this, and are living it. And day by day you struggle to find the reasons for living.

Most of you know that, however dark and hollow you might feel inside, you won't actually commit suicide. If only because you could never do that to the people that care about you, never hurt them like that—and hurt them you would, to incredible extremes, and those scars would be permanent. Trust me, people do really care about you. Sadly, it often doesn't become extremely obvious until we're dead, and then it can also be rather hard to tell, on account of being six feet under. A bit of a Catch-22.

Perhaps you don't kill yourself because you're scared of what comes next. Your fear of life might be great *(what more fresh hells are yet to come?!)* but fear of death is indefatigable, inescapable. We fear most what we don't know and don't understand. Oh, it's one thing to fantasize about, but it's quite another thing to be faced with it, for it to suddenly be all too real. Sometimes our fear of life *is* our fear of death—our fear that our lives won't be enough, that it'll all end no matter what we do, that one by one everyone gets snuffed out like a candle . . .

Ironically, our fear of death causes us to delay and put off actually living our own lives. Saying "live every day like it was your last" is all very well, but when death is a vague constant in your mind, a spectre hanging over you, you hardly have much get-up-and-go. In actual fact, living each day like it was your last would be incredibly depressing, and eventually terribly boring. Think of all those funeral arrangements to make every day! And you'd wind everyone up by constantly saying your last goodbyes.

Maybe you don't kill yourself because you still have some last vestige of hope: hope in the world, hope in others, hope in your own potential. Or because killing yourself can be quite a bit of effort, when all's said and done.

Knowing you'll never take the plunge doesn't make it any easier— in fact, that makes it worse. The comprehension that you will have to stick it out until the final whistle blows can be overwhelming,

I just fell down a flight of stairs in real life and in my head

exhausting in its misery. Seeing the wasteland spread out before you, disappearing over the horizon, can feel like the ultimate gunshot of depression—a torture with no end in sight, an infinity of shit.

You're not alone.

I'm fairly confident (kill me if I'm wrong—no, wait—) that I at least won't make you any worse. But, ultimately, the strength is in you. You've made it this far, so I know without a shadow of a doubt that you're strong. And that tells me that I know you're going to keep going. What you're looking for, I think, is a reason why you should.

So let's see what we can do.

"But I, being poor, have only my dreams; I have spread my dreams under your feet; Tread softly because you tread on my dreams."

—William Butler Yeats

CYNICAL SELF-HELP

Most self-help books are garbage. There, I said it. Few diehard depressives and cynics worth their salt will pick up one of those fluffy-minded books that wax lyrical about the power of positive thinking and brightening up every day, bombarding you with inane truisms, horrifically naïve observations, and trite, misguided advice.

Such things are Kryptonite to the imaginative pessimist, what sunshine is to Dracula, and there is much in the way of literature and studies to support the idea that this enforced clinging to everything positive and dismissing everything negative actually does more harm than good. Bad things do happen. Life isn't all roses and never will be. "Negative" feelings will always be around and often for good reason. In fact, "negative" emotions should not simply be squashed out. They are important and—a lot of the time—deserve to be heard. Try to ignore them, and you're just letting them fester—until one day they've risen up so strong inside that they form a coup and entirely crush you.

It's dangerous to indulge in blind optimism. It's insulting—to yourself as well as others. There are very real problems people have, sometimes small (but still important and still deserving of acknowledgment) and sometimes huge and devastating. Problems, real problems, must be dealt with or overcome—never ignored, never brushed off.

Tell me, when you have a major problem, when you're suffering in some way, who would you rather turn to: a blind optimist with a permanent smile, or a realist who battles their own problems? I don't know about you, but I wouldn't feel comfortable trying to argue my case for why I'm justified in feeling bad with somebody who tries to wipe my mood slate clean and repaint it with kittens and bunnies in hats. If I'm going to talk to anyone, it's someone who accepts the way I'm feeling and doesn't try to dismiss it— ideally somebody who's been there themselves.

There's no amount of rainbows and sunshine that can help. Getting that pushed on you from all sides by a society wearing rose-tinted glasses will only embitter and isolate you further. A further wedge will be driven. You'll feel even more that there's something wrong with you—because your darker emotions are treated like a disease, and not part and parcel of your humanity.

Both you and other people are allowed to have negative emotions. You're allowed to express hurt, and pain, and fear, and misery, and grief. You're allowed to feel that you want to die. We want to try to diminish those feelings, but to do that we *must* acknowledge their existence and that they exist for a reason.

"Believe it, and it will come true." Okay, here goes. *I believe I can fly.* *Takes the leap.*

Oh. I see. Thanks for that, I've just broken both my legs.

The universe doesn't give a shit about your positive thinking. It won't respond to it. You might be lucky or you might not be. The universe is just as likely to send a meteorite your way as it is to obey your every singing, Disney-like command.

Self-help authors (not all of them) spout these things for two reasons. One is money, obviously, because they're easy for many types of people to lap up, even though most of what's written in the book is painfully transparent, and painfully repetitive, and

could be thought of by anybody if they just stopped and thought for an hour (or had a bit of a google), and the rest is simply bad advice. The other is because they are of the sun-is-always-shining personality type, with the accompanying conviction that these things work. And perhaps they do, to these targeted types of people, for whom their depression, disillusion, and despair is just a bad, bewildering patch in an otherwise glass-is-half-full life, and not their very state of existence, something they've grown up accepting and understanding.

Chances are, excuse my cynicism, the people for whom these books work best are not even depressed but are just feeling lost and directionless and under the weather, like we might feel on a day we'd consider "all right, actually." They're given page-by-page reassuring pats on the back and a series of "things to do each day" like pet a cat and smell some flowers or whatever, and then they go and post a five star review on Amazon.

I'd tell you I'm not a bitter person, but I'd be lying.

I'm hoping that's why you're still reading.

So, now that I've unfairly alienated all my peers, is this a self-help book? Urgh. If you can imagine a cynic like me (here's a drinking game: drink every time you see the words "cynic," "depressed," and "pessimist"—game not suitable for alcoholics) writing a self-help book and not wanting to go to the store to buy more rope, then okay, this is a self-help book.

Shoot me now.

In fact, I'm committing self-flagellation just to try to make up for the fact that this book is technically a self-help guide and would no doubt be stored in the same section in bookstores. It might actually touch those other fluffy books. I can't help it, I feel dirty.

But I want to do more than just give you a few pats on the back and call it a day. The last thing I want to do is patronize you, or dismiss your cynicism. I want to sink into this with you, just to show that I think I understand where at least some of you are coming from. I know the blackness. I know the emptiness. I'm on first name terms with The Void (It's Barry, for the record).

Okay, let's not call this self-help, let's keep calling it a Survival Guide. Then I'm more like Ray Mears or Bear Grylls (except not anywhere near as capable).

After all, it's not that you're simply trying to help yourself. You have a far more important and grueling task at hand. You're trying to survive.

HOW DARE YOU, SUICIDE ISN'T FUNNY

"If I had no sense of humor, I would long ago have committed suicide." –Mahatma Gandhi

The title of this book, *How Not to Kill Yourself,* came before I'd written a word. I knew it was perfect as soon as I thought of it. I don't think the book would have gained any attention at all if not for the title.

I *want* you to find it funny. I really do. Okay, I know it's not really *ha-ha* funny. But when people ask me about this book, the title makes it a little easier. *How Not to Kill Yourself,* I say, and I give them a big grin, bordering on a laugh. They grin in return, maybe even chuckle. A little uncomfortable, sure, that's to be expected. I still wouldn't say it's easy. With some people, it never will be. After all, this is about suicide as much as it's about depression. But for the people I most want to talk to about this, I think it's easier. I want them to find it amusing, sardonic, strange, inappropriate. It's offbeat and I like that. People don't quite know how to react, so I grin or laugh to let them know it's okay. We can talk about it, it's okay.

The more we can laugh, the more we can relax, the more we can talk, the more we can admit to ourselves, admit as a nation, admit as a world that men and women (especially men: the silent sex, the suicide sex) are killing themselves at ever more alarming rates.

I want it to be easier.

Perhaps you don't agree. Maybe you are disgruntled by the title, still, and you're reading this (and boiling up over the mordant, tongue-in-cheek way I write about this incredibly sensitive issue) in order to fuel your self-righteousness. Don't worry, I get it. That's not me judging you. I do similar things.

But not over humor.

I'm guessing that a good number of you are still alive today thanks to your sense of humor. It can, in fact, be the strongest thing there is.

No, not "can." It *is*.

Some people say those who laugh at death are sick. Jokes can be sick, of course, especially when it comes to black comedy and shock humor, but it simply does not follow that the *joker* is sick (there are much better ways of telling if somebody is a bad egg).

Jokes *defang*. They rob power from things that hurt us. There's that old adage: if you take life too seriously, you'll never get out alive. You've heard it a lot, no doubt, but it's still perfectly true. Humor will put its hands on its hips and stare these monsters head-on and sap their strength. In Stephen King's *It*, the hideous eponymous antagonist—the stuff of nightmares—is terribly afraid of and weakened by the children's laughter, because it robs It of It's power, of It's ability to feed on their fear.

If there is anything out there that, no matter the quality and punchiness of the joke, you could never laugh at (and would be disgusted at yourself if you did), then that thing is *taboo*. What that means is that it is special, that it is an exception, and, following from that, it therefore has a certain power over you. That power is born of fear.

At university, I had a friend whose father died suddenly. I saw her maybe a week later at a bar. She made a joke about her father dying. It wasn't a ha-ha knock-knock kind of joke. The punchline was my reaction. I could see the delight in her face, as she reveled for a few seconds in my discomfort, confusion, astonishment, and amusement. What could I say? How was I supposed to react? We both knew there were no rules to govern something like this, and there was no rebuttal, no witticism I could have—nor should have—made.

I could see immediately what she'd gained, what we'd all gained in that moment. In private, in her own personal space, she would still be grieving—immeasurably so. But in the here and now she laughed at me, and the world relaxed. She wasn't a victim, not right then. If you are going through an awful time—whether it be bereavement, depression, mental illness, or indeed anything—then people will walk around you on eggshells. Your presence will make people uncomfortable. It's not right, but that's how it is. Very few people are good at dealing with someone who is going through great upset. Many will drape you in sympathy, bombard you with it. Sorry after sorry after sorry. And "Can I help?" and "I'm here for you if you need me." As long as you allow yourself to be viewed as nothing but a sympathy case, nothing but a victim, you will cement yourself in it. It will come to be all you are.

She laughed. We laughed. We knew there was still something dark and cruel in that room, but it had been banished to the corners. It was not the thing itself, merely a spectre of the thing. It had been robbed of its power, for an hour or two.

You can still accept people's sympathies without letting them define you. You can control the situation. You can choose how the outside world will handle you. There will be a great many times where you don't want to be treated like somebody who is bereaved, somebody who is depressed, somebody who is ill, somebody who is suicidal. Encourage others—leading by example—to treat you like the old you, or even a *new* you—as long as it's a *whole* you;

not simply somebody enslaved to their troubles and woe, or a collection of issues in human form, but a person capable of smiles and laughter, capable of friendship. When others know they can treat you bigger, treat you *normal*, when they can separate you from your troubles for a time, then the opportunity arises for them to act in a way that will lighten you further.

Try not to be precious about anything, especially the things that hurt you. You are not a fragile flower. You are bold and brilliant and savage when you need to be. You too can banish spectres to the corners of rooms, to the cracks in the walls, to the clouds in the sky. You can find relief everywhere, and in everyone.

Don't be so afraid of these horrible things. It's okay. It's okay to laugh them back into the darkness. Anybody who says otherwise are . . . well, let's be honest, they're just fucktrumpets.

Everyone I've ever known and cared about might spontaneously combust, all in one go, and (providing I still have my cookies and cake) I'd still want you to come up to me and remind me it's okay to laugh. I might punch you in the face, but you should say it to me anyway.

Of course, you probably shouldn't go up to anyone else facing something awful and tell them that it's okay to laugh. That's my job. I can say it to you because you're reading this somewhere and hopefully I'm way too far away for you to punch me.

Laughter really *is* the best medicine, and there are no strict lines to be drawn for its use. You shouldn't assume you understand why someone is joking about something. And you should never, ever rob somebody of their sense of humor, for you might just be taking away their lifeline.

Suicide is taboo, and because it is taboo we don't talk about it.

We should talk about it. You should talk about it. The more people that talk about it openly, and that both follows on from and precludes making jokes about it (a good joke never undermines the seriousness of a singular tragic event, and sometimes actually underlines it—in fact, good jokes are, more often than not, not targeting specific, personal tragedies, but are almost entirely fictionalized), the more we can understand it, the more we can empathize, the more we can help each other. The more we can teach each other how not to kill ourselves.

SO... IT'S ALL A BIT SHIT REALLY, ISN'T IT?

*"There were days when she was unhappy, she did not know why—
when it did not seem worthwhile to be glad or sorry, to be alive or
dead; when life appeared to her like a grotesque pandemonium
and humanity like worms struggling blindly toward inevitable
annihilation."* —Kate Chopin

The world is awful.

It's a subjective statement, and therefore frequently quite wrong, but there's no denying that sometimes, on some days (and for some of us on far too many days), it seems as plain as the nose on your face. You're ten thousand leagues beyond fed up, you're horribly lonely—and when you're with someone, you just want them to fuck off.

If you're living with a partner (or family, or roommates), you're feeling sour and frustrated with them, not with anything particular they've done, just with their very presence. You know how unreasonable you're being, but you feel it anyway. You'd give

I'd ask you on a date but I don't think you'd want to spend 2 hours in silence sitting next to me staring at a blank wall

anything to be on your own, to be given some goddamn space for once.

If you're living alone, and don't have somebody, you're bitter in your loneliness, and would give anything to have a partner who could comfort you and watch crappy films and love you. Except, buried very deep down, you know that if this person was to suddenly come into your life, it'd take no time at all before you were thinking, *what fresh hell is this?* and *I was happier when I was by myself.* Which might be bullshit, and you might recognize it as bullshit, but really all that happened was you'd displaced one unhappiness with another species of unhappiness—but both species come from the same family tree, and your utter disgust with life is still there.

You look on Facebook, at your awful friends (if you have any— *Can I really call them my friends?* you wonder) with their awful lives, posting their awful vacuous crap about how awfully happy things are for them. You see comments on articles from blogs and online news sites (actively seeking out clickbait that'll annoy you the most), and you scroll through all the most inane comments and their replies, fouling your mind (with a certain grim satisfaction) at the inherent shittiness of humanity—that at its best is merely ignorant and at its worst is offensively tragic, or tragically offensive.

You're better than these people—but that's kind of a positive feeling, so you don't dwell on it, but push it away.

You receive a message or somebody says something to you in person. It's short, brusque. Maybe they don't say anything at all, maybe it's just the way they looked at you just then. What did they mean by it? Are they angry? Are they angry at you? Why are they in a mood? What have you done wrong (apart from everything, ever)? You might otherwise treat it as nothing, or at least consider it ambiguous . . . but no, they're definitely frustrated with you, sick of you. You torture yourself by overthinking it, inventing reasons for them to be upset with you, making it worse and worse in your head. To them, it was probably nothing. Already forgotten. To you, it's just one more symptom.

Technology decides to take this moment to fuck with you. Expect to encounter incomprehensible error messages, and the temporary death of your internet connection. Your phone, your computer, your router—you see them all laughing at you. When you finally get back online (which had absolutely nothing to do with your many efforts to restore it) you stare blankly at all the awful things happening in the world. The political circus. The wars, the poverty. Obnoxious individuals in their fifteen minutes to fifteen years of fame. But, somehow worse than all of that put together is the infinite stupidity of ordinary people, observed so clearly in all directions, as though the internet were a window to some Victorian freak show. Humanity seeming some sad carnival act that repeats itself over and over and over until the end of time and nobody learns anything, ever.

Everything is horrible and stupid, and you thought that'd be bad enough, but it isn't. The color is starting to drain from everything. You cease to even care. The stupidity, the irrational hatred everywhere, it's all obvious, expected, mundane.

Everything becomes empty and lifeless.

You manage to summon the energy to move your head to look out the window at the slate gray sky, at the bones in the trees aching from the cruel wind. The weather reflects your soul.

Hyperbole suits you, right now. You envision a big red button with "End all human life" stamped on it. You imagine pressing it and remembering what it felt like to actually, genuinely smile—albeit for the last time.

DOGS, SWAMPS, AND BLANKETS

The most common metaphor for depression might be the image of the big black dog. I've also seen it excellently represented, in a comic by Sylvie Reuter, as a pitch-black figure like a living shadow that sits on the shoulder. It gets bigger and bigger (and scarier) in every panel, until the whole panel is in blackness.

Right now, I'm thinking of depression in two different ways.

The first is a swamp, one that seems to go on forever. Depression is, when you are in it, less of a single controlling entity, or even part of you, but rather a landscape, a world you are living in.

It's also not consistent. Just because you are depressed does not necessarily mean you are exactly the same day in, day out. The swamp changes as you move through it. Sometimes it's not so bad. You can just about find your footing, you haven't tripped over any fallen branches lately and gotten a face full of muck . . . and is that sunlight up ahead? Well, sort of, I mean it's the faintest sliver . . . but it's something . . . What is that? Is that the end of the swamp?! Oh, no, not really, but that doesn't mean it's not an improvement on the previous bit . . .

Sometimes it's really bad. You're sinking with every step, and you barely keep your head above water. Where's the dry land? Does it even exist? It's so cold and dark . . .

Depression is a swamp because it subtly evolves, it changes. It's a delicately balanced ecosystem, where every little thing affects something else. Crowding trees and vines and darkness obscure what else might be out there. It seems endless, but it's not. It seems abjectly awful, but it isn't. There's life in a swamp. There's hope. It's small and it's wild, and it's as apt to run away from you as it is to approach you, but it's there. It's real.

The only one worse than me is everyone else

My second visualization of depression is a black blanket in winter. This is the kind of idea that people who haven't been depressed are unlikely to understand. You see, depression can be, dare I say it, comforting. I'm not saying that's a reason to keep it up—just because something is comforting doesn't mean it's good for you. But when you are deep in depression, you don't want help. You even, in a vague, unspoken way, are *content* to stay within it. You have a kind of sour self-satisfaction with how things are. You gather a kind of uniform cynical feeling about everything, and anything that challenges that perception is wrong, stupid, useless, and pathetic.

Outside, the world is cold and hard and bitter. The blanket of depression protects you. It even warms you. *I'm fine*, you say. You'd scowl or sneer if you had the energy. *I have my blanket.*

YOU WOULDN'T LIKE ME WHEN I'M ANGRY

Depression is different for everybody, and so nobody can really explain it perfectly for you, but there is enough in common to hit a general mark. It makes great bedfellows with similar words beginning with D—disillusion, despair, disgust, degradation (of your personality, your attitude, your body, the state of your bedroom).

Other words, too, cuddle up to depression, words like apathy and laziness. Not your ordinary, basic apathy and laziness, oh no, these are mega shit-ton ACME anvils of apathy and laziness that flatten you into the ground with their irrepressible weight. If you get it bad, this is the kind of laziness that will make it not only a supreme effort of will to get up to go to the toilet or get yourself a drink, but also a supreme effort of will to turn your head ninety degrees.

If you get it bad, this is the kind of apathy where you will not only not give a shit about people you don't know falling sick and dying in the world, but also the miseries of people you *do* know, the troubles of people who may well be in your company right now, troubles that you might yourself be causing them right this second. I know myself what it's like to see somebody you love stand beside you crying because of how you're being, and have the sheer inability to care.

The guilt you feel when these blackest of clouds have passed does not stop you from being like this again.

However, there's one emotion I haven't mentioned yet. And that's because it's the only one that is redeemable. That emotion is anger.

Sadness and despair and the like are very passive, lethargic feelings. It is a good, rewarding and constructive thing to cry sometimes—and I'd always recommend that over stewing in your own emotional numbness—but with depression, sadness more times than not doesn't lead to crying, and that's when you have even more cause to worry. Or, perhaps, you cry so often that it's lost all meaning and reward, and finishing one bout doesn't make you feel any better, but simply is the prelude to the next bout.

Anger, however, is not so much a passive emotion, even if its activity is usually constrained to circling the mind's pit like a snarling panther. Anger—and do not confuse this with hate, which can be passive, and is uniformly ugly—does not let you lie down, barely taking the time to blink and breathe, feeling utterly *woe is me*. No, anger pumps your blood, it makes you tremble, it distorts your face, it gives you *energy*; it destroys that numbness and makes you feel.

Sure, that feeling is generally viewed as "negative," but that doesn't necessarily mean it's always bad for you. Sometimes, it's a matter of the better of two evils. You can utilize that anger as the first step out of your depression, as well as to defy the appeal of suicide. Use that anger, just do not abuse that anger. Do not take this anger out on anyone (unless they really, really, *really* deserve it—and then it's best to confine it to simply shouting unless you want to be depressed in jail, where they are notoriously stingy with their cookies). Put your anger on a leash and make it submit to you.

What should I be angry about if I can't take it out on someone else, you might ask? You might tell me that you're already angry about a lot of stupid things in the world and in your life. That guy Joe, for instance, just the other day said to you . . . and then he had the *audacity* to . . .

The anger I want to arouse in you, and be cultivated, has an end goal—and that end goal is stubbornness.

If you're already a stubborn person (are you? Be honest now, most imaginative pessimists are stubborn in some way, such as a stubbornness in not following the rules and going their own way) then great, this shouldn't be too hard.

Anger can lead to stubbornness because anger is an aspect of self-preservation. It's a combative stance, and it requires something to rail against. To be angry requires you to elevate yourself above this other thing. It requires at least a small sense of superiority (even if you're only angry at yourself—that's one part of you feeling stronger and smarter and more worthwhile than another, less valued part).

Stubbornness is anger settled down a little and given a hot cup of tea, given time to cement and reflect upon itself. Time to dig its heels in. *I'm not budging*, it says. *That's wrong, and unfair, and I'm right.*

Stubbornness is ego. Ego and stubbornness aren't always great. They can stop people taking meds. They can stop people asking for or accepting help. They can make people unsympathetic to others. They can make people blind to their own faults and to those times where they themselves really *are* in the wrong.

But it can also be a force for good, a defensive force, a barrier against the hurt and unfairness of the world.

Ego and self-awareness should always be a balance, keeping each other in check.

We'll return to ego later on. Because, like you, it's a Pretty Big Deal.

OH NO YOU DIDN'T

Here's the thing I want you to consider.

How dare the world lead you to actually contemplate killing yourself? That's fucking horrific. The world should be utterly ashamed. Every single thing that has—outside of your own control—contributed in some way to this completely tragic state of affairs, is in fact part of an unintentional collaboration that ends (or would, if they had it their way, the bastards) in your death. That is, at the very least, involuntary manslaughter.

Some people say that blaming the outside world for everything instead of holding yourself responsible is unhealthy.

But it's not our end goal. And—I'll only say this once—I don't actually expect you to take this 100% seriously, not in your rational mind. But I'm not appealing to your rational mind, I'm appealing to your ego, to your emotion, your inner stubbornness, your sense of survival, and perhaps even to your dramatic sense of theatrics.

In short, blaming the world is a very useful means to an end.

Let's say it again. How dare the world take you to this precipice? I hope you'll join me in agreeing how very wrong it is. And it's not just you. All over the world people are killing themselves, taking lives full of potential and throwing them away—all because the nature of the world led them to it.

That is disgusting.

And you know what? I won't stand for it. I won't let it lead me by the rope. I won't kowtow to the executioner. I won't sign my own death warrant, especially in a kangaroo court in which the jury was clearly hand picked and the judge has been heavily bribed. Now that I think about it, where was my defense counsel? Where's my attorney-for-life? Hell, I didn't even sign up for this freak show! I never filled out no goddamn consent form before I was brought into this world! I didn't ask for any of this!

I'm not going to bend over and let the world fuck me like this, and I hope you won't either. I want you to see the travesty in it, the ridiculousness, the sheer nerve, and I want you to get angry that it really has come to this. I mean, you tried, you really *tried*—and wasn't it awful?—and yet your efforts have been spat back in your face.

You don't *really* want to kill yourself—you're letting the world force your hand.

Well, I'm not going to let them win. And you should join me.

Don't let the world win.

Don't let it keep robbing great people and dumping them in the bin of history.

We can put a stop to it. We can be the first to say NO!—or better yet, FUCK OFF!

Stand tall, stand straight, and tell the world where to go. This is one soul it's not going to crush. You are stronger than that. You can FIGHT BACK.

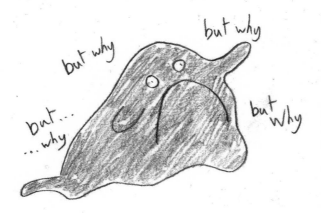

THE DEATH OF POTENTIAL

Think of all the people, good and great, all the visionaries, all the imaginative pessimists who have been lost to themselves because of this cruel, heartless world. People like Sylvia Plath and Robert E. Howard, Hunter S. Thompson and Kurt Cobain, Tony Hancock and Vincent Van Gogh, Alexander McQueen and Ian Curtis, Robin Williams and Virginia Woolf, David Foster Wallace and Gérard de Nerval, Ernest Hemingway and Chester Bennington and Chris Cornell. It goes on and on. And those are just the famous ones.

Too much has been lost. No more. I'm angry, and you should be too.

Let the anger move to stubbornness, stubbornness in the face of life and all its adversity. Let your thoughts move to *not this time sonny*, and *I'll show you*, and end on *I've got some stuff to prove, just you wait*.

Don't extinguish your potential before it's even begun to develop.

Because that's what they'll be saying about you afterwards, I assure you. S/he had such potential. Such a shame. Such a waste.

You know, you'll never get a second chance, a chance to try again. Hovering over the funeral thinking *hmm, they might have a point there*, and *wow, all these people are actually really sad about this, how odd, makes you kinda feel regret*, and *better jump back a week and see what I can do to turn this ship around.*

I'm sure you've imagined your own suicide enough times; you don't need me to ask you to do so again. Likewise, when we're morbid, funerals are always a "fun" thing to imagine in painstaking detail.

Let me guess . . . something like an overdose, or a gun to the head/ in the mouth, a hanging rope (old-school), a big fall? All been done countless times. I thought you were special?

Sorry, sorry, that's my job—you ARE special! There's only one of you, for crying out loud! The world will never—NEVER—see the likes of you again. Not just you, but all the things you could give back to the world!

Okay, the world, as we've established, doesn't deserve your work, given that the world is a raging bastard (for now, seeing as we're still being stubborn here). And people en masse might not deserve it. But the world is full of good and great individuals, many of them people like you—other imaginative pessimists—and they *need* you, just as you need them.

All those books never written, all those paintings never painted, all those songs never sung.

And there you are, ended before you began. In your death throes. Flapping like a fish at the feet of your own ego. What a limp end to such a life.

I don't want to go out like that, and I bet you don't either. I want to go out tough, like the toughest damn cookie anybody's ever tried to eat.

An ideal death, of course, is by choice—but certainly not an early one, not one before all is said and done. I'd like to go out aged 112 in a ship explosion while being targeted by ninja assassins, or stabbed twelve times by boarding pirates. I'd like to go out like Boromir in Lord of the Rings, except with more arrows. I'd like to go out like a martyr, saving the world from some alien catastrophe by being the one to press some big red apocalyptic button, a feat only made possible by my heroic self-sacrifice, for which all the world will remember me (and believe me, I'd milk that scene for everything it's worth). I'd like to go out by having a cardiac arrest in bed with a dozen skilled nymphomaniacs, some of them still brushing stray specks of cocaine off their bodies as the police and ambulance arrive, the police arriving first thanks to the noise complaints caused by a wall-shaking volume of hard

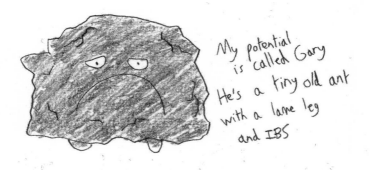

My potential is called Gary
He's a tiny old ant
with a lame leg
and IBS

rock that aggressively ushered me to my signing out of this world. That's assuming I have any complaining neighbors on my private tropical pirate island.

Sorry.

I'm not, really.

Dying in a puddle of piss and tears having half-vomited my overdose back, likely spending four hours dying in a hospital in intense agony due to my own inability to do the job properly? Firing the wrong gun at the wrong part of my head and spending the rest of my life comatose and dribbling and unable to communicate, "switch me off you bastards?" Jumping off a bridge that wasn't high enough and cracking my legs, spending the rest of my life in a wheelchair unable to do anything for myself and yet cared for/

guarded every second of the day, thus forever preventing me from a "let's try that again?"

Fuck. Off.

Let's take a time-out from the thrust of all this rhetoric, and give you some tips of the trade (the trade being a Professional Miserable Bastard—PMB).

SOME PRACTICAL TIPS

O ne day a wanderer was out wandering, when he fell off a cliff. Sort of. I mean, he grabbed hold at the last minute, halfway down the cliff-face, and somehow didn't break both his wrists. They must have been really strong for some reason. Anyway, as it turns out, this was Tiger Country (he hadn't bothered to read the signs). So some hungry tigers came to the top of the cliff and looked down at him. He assumed they were hungry because their falling dribble kept hitting him in the face. He looked to the side for a better handhold, and saw a perfect cake balanced in a little nook—not just a slice, a whole, delicious cake—wrapped up in plastic wrap. Weird. Maybe a really big bird had left it. He prodded it and saw that it was soft and fresh. He looked up and saw the dribbling tigers. He looked down and saw a smooth, slippery rock face that seemed to go on forever. It seemed there was certain death above and below (and nowhere to climb to the sides either, in case you were wondering that, clever clogs). And he'd forgotten to pack his climbing tools (for the same reason he hadn't read the warning signs: because he was *a complete dolt). What the hell should I do? he asked himself, and he thought for a minute, as the ache in his fingers grew and more tigers joined the pack.*

In the end, he just ate the cake. It was hella tasty.

—Ancient Buddhist parable (adapted by me)

VIDEO GAMES

I'm serious. There's a lot of evidence these days that video games can help fight depression, and I've noticed the effect repeatedly myself. Perhaps you don't like video games—although I should stress that they're not all mindless violent shoot-em-ups, they come in ALL shapes and sizes, just like movies, from the by-the-book to the fantastically creative. Except, unlike movies, the medium itself comes in many different forms. From shooters to strategy games, from wacky puzzle games to home improvement simulations. The way you engage with these games is entirely different with each one. I'm personally rather addicted to playing the *Traveller's Tales* licensed Lego video games co-op with my partner. You can die countless times in a row and it doesn't matter one little bit. There's something relaxing and encouraging about that.

I'm sure you don't need me to tell you about video games, though. You're hip. But really—I guess it's the mixture of distraction

I like to make the worst possible decisions for my character just to see if I can make their life worse than mine

and escapism coupled with manageable challenges and easy productivity that makes them work. They can be as creative and as carefully designed as a movie, leading you by the hand, but they also require mild concentration and active involvement that a movie doesn't, and so rouse you from your stupor without actually asking much of you. Give it a try, unless you hate all video games with a passion. One suggestion though—don't play a game so "challenging" (read: frustrating) that it'll make you throw a gamepad/keyboard/phone against the wall.

"Couch co-op," aka offline split-screen games (that means playing with someone else sitting next to you), are great for sharing time with somebody that you wouldn't be doing things with otherwise (because of being depressed, lazy, uncommunicative, and wanting them to fuck off). You both get something out of it. Who knows? At the end of the level you might even be speaking to them.

If you're stuck, try LEGO Pirates. And no, sadly, I wasn't paid to say that.

The key part of all this being . . .

PRODUCTIVITY

"No artist is ever morbid. The artist can express everything."

- Oscar Wilde, *The Portrait of Dorian Gray*

Now, this is something fairly impossible to do during hard depressive episodes, but if you're just feeling generally shitty in life, but are still able to, y'know, move about and function like a normal human being for a spell (perhaps wading in a milder patch of swamp), then you owe it to yourself (in more ways than one) to be productive during that time.

And by productive I don't just mean with video games, but also creatively so (although there are other effective ways to be productive—including grocery shopping or doing the dishes). Get that imagination of yours out of your head and into the material world. Express yourself. Even if you think it'll be shit. It doesn't matter, you just need to open the spout and get it flowing.

Write, draw, whatever. It can be anything, it can be nothing. You could just put the pen on the paper and let it waggle around. It might become something. If you're inspired—even if it's just a little inspiration—use it. If there's a project of your own you could be working on, work on it. Nothing might come out, and that's okay. Don't give up instantly. Don't beat yourself up about it. Part of you might actually *want* to fail, just so you can be more miserable with yourself. *I told you so,* you'll say, with a face like a mashed potato. But it's alright, really. Try again later, try again tomorrow. It doesn't matter. If it comes it comes. If it doesn't at least you tried. At least you focused on something else. But know that it doesn't have to be anything *proper*. Create freely, without restraints or even purpose. Tap those keys and see what comes out. It really doesn't matter.

Write about yourself, how you're feeling, how you're not feeling. Exaggerate it beyond belief, make it poetry, use the highest levels

I wrote a book once.
It was called
"Things I Think Are Great"
and it was
200 blank pages

of hyperbole. Make it cataclysmic, apocalyptic. It's yours to own, you can express it however you wish—the more cathartic, the better. Take that storm in your head and write it or draw it as a physical storm. Draw yourself in the pain you are in. You don't have to create nice things. Some of the most incredible and powerful things ever made are not in the slightest bit *nice*.

You don't have to create nice things, and you're not duty-bound to show people anything you do. It can be shared, or it can be just for yourself. You can have a whole world of things just for you, that nobody can ever see or touch or know about.

Look outside. Look at the trees, at the moon. Look at the people. Don't see them for what they are, see them for what they *could* be. Imagine them as something else. Imagine them how you want to see them. However surreal or fantastical or scary or sad or dangerous. Take the time to think about them like that. Create them like that. Do this often, do this always. This will not only help you appreciate the world around you more, and open up your perspectives, it will also bolster your imagination and blow little bursts of oxygen onto your creative spark. But more than that, it'll put you on fonder terms with your own mind, and all the things it's capable of.

Write. Draw. Paint. Photograph. Film. Animate. Perform. Craft. Sculpt. Construct. Sew. Cook. Design. Experiment. Edit. Program. Plan. Blog. Brainstorm. Vent. Imagine.

Think. Create. Play.

When you have ended a day with something to show for it, however small, however silly, you will feel quite a bit less shit than if you didn't.

That's how it begins. And you're in it for the long game.

GO OUTSIDE

An obvious one this, that everybody else is sure to be telling you. I know it's an effort, and I'm not saying to try to do it when you're in a complete stupor of apathy and lethargy (maybe even considering thinking about trying to do it will make you hate me, and actually doing it might be like running into a train). But if you're down but not quite out, go outside for a walk. Night walks are often good, because you're not so disturbed by cars and other people and the sun isn't trying to wriggle under your eyelids like they were duvets in order to have sex with your eyes.

Be alone with your thoughts, but in fresh air. Ooh that fresh air! If you can find woods or a park, or somewhere at least half-heartedly nature-lite, go there. Especially at night, when you won't be so busy judging other humans.

Go off the beaten path. Go in unfamiliar directions and find new places. Explore.

Night walks are also good because if you're depressed and not working, chances are you're getting up too late to give the sun much more than a hello-goodbye.

Maybe bring headphones.

And music. Not just headphones by themselves.

MUSIC

"Who hears music, feels his solitude peopled at once."

–Robert Browning

Music is an interesting one, and people will always disagree on it.

I find silence heavy and depressing, and it grows the longer it goes on. To me, silence is one of the worst things there is, especially for depression. It provides zero buffer against your own thoughts.

Don't pick something really happy (you'll hate it) and don't pick something suicidally depressing, for obvious reasons. I used to have an album I nicknamed "the suicide album," because it was so brutally, relentlessly soul-crushing that listening to it was like scraping myself with razors. I still have the album, but I don't listen to it anymore. On the very rare occasions in the past when it was played, you knew shit was serious. I'm not entirely sure whether it helped or not. I guess it was those moments when I really wanted to wallow in misery. Maybe I got it out of my system or maybe it just made me feel worse.

These days, the band I listen to when I'm down but not out (and, admittedly, a lot of the rest of the time too) is the little-known gothic/doom country of Those Poor Bastards. I'm not trying to promote them to you (well, maybe a little), because most people won't like them, but I want to explain why they're my choice above any other.

Those Poor Bastards has, to me, the perfect balance. Their music is dark, sorrowful, dour and bitter, and yet it also carries a tongue-in-cheek self-awareness of it all, a kind of happiness-in-misery that comes out and makes it entertaining. And I dig the accent and the atmosphere. I love to sing along to it all (the low notes are ideal for my register when I'm glum), and the lyrics are easily relatable. You start out with minimum-effort mumbling, then

I'd tell you to play Hurt by Johnny Cash but it's just too happy

moaning, and then before you know it you're almost having fun singing along. The music and lyrics are sad and supremely pessimistic, sardonic, cathartic, and even bleakly amusing all at once. I mean, how could I resist such opening lines to the aptly titled "God Damned Me" as *"If you wanna see a man with a lot of bad luck, honey just look over at me"*?

After singing along to TPB, I might feel just about okay enough to sing along to other things. And that's the staircase up and out.

I'm not saying TPB will work for you. Chances are it won't. But you'll find your own ideal music, if you haven't already. Music that is neither painfully joyful nor wholly, uniformly miserable. Introspective, relatable music, about the human things we all feel from time to time. Music which understands you at that point in time, without committing to making you feel even worse. If you can bring yourself to sing along, all the better.

If you only ever listen to super happy or superficial party music, you might want to have a look elsewhere for alternatives. Someone I knew used to listen to ABBA when he was miserable and depressed. I can't think of anything worse.

Possibly silence.

GET DRESSED

This is *much* easier than going outside. Don't spend all your days in just a robe, or lounge pants, or pajamas. Wearing such things all day is the very antithesis of a call to action. It's a call to laziness and apathy and it will keep you in your stupor. That doesn't mean you can't still have relaxing days while wearing proper clothes— but you will feel at least mildly better doing it.

I'm not saying getting dressed is going to end your depression. But it is that very small aid that you need every single day. You will feel that tiny bit better and more useful if you make sure you're fully dressed every day. You are far more likely to push yourself into doing other things, into being productive in some small or significant way.

You're more likely to say "yes" to things if you're already wearing clothes.

You will also look better to yourself in the mirror, which is important for your state of mind. Don't throw on any old rubbish, just because you know you don't have to leave the house. Dress up as often as you can in some of your favorite clothes, whether you're leaving the house or not. This is just for you. Who cares if nobody else really sees them? You're hardly wearing them out just being in the house. But it's a hell of a lot better than wearing clothes more suitable for a coma.

If you come home from work (or some other tiring activity) exhausted and want to slip into your pajamas straight away, okay, sure, we all like comfort and lying around with our legs splayed out all over the furniture. But if it's a long-standing habit, then maybe try to wean yourself off from doing it all the time. Get changed of course, nobody wants to keep wearing work clothes—but change into something nice! You're too cool not to!

Actually, there's a bigger suggestion to be made here . . .

LOOK AFTER YOURSELF (AND FIGHT THE DARK SIDE)

Depression and suicidal thoughts are like the Dark Side of the Force (from the *Star Wars* films, for the three people in the world who didn't know). They'll try to pull at you, they'll try to grow on you and envelop you. The Dark Side feeds on a person's fear and hate. Depression feeds on fear too, but it also feeds on an unhealthy mind and body, on insecurity, on a sense of ugliness and distaste. It wants you to sink into its swamp.

What you need to do is put up as many barriers as possible against the pull of depression and these horrible thoughts. I want you to take away some of the things they can feed on, things that are easy enough to fix. Simple, everyday practical things that are even easier to ignore as you sink into an apathetic stupor.

Sleep is like being dead but without the commitment

Things like keeping a window open to let some fresh air in. If you're chilly, add more layers if possible before you close the window. Again, if it's not too much to ask, go outside for a spell—even if it's only for a few minutes. Breathe deeply.

Try to maintain a not-totally-abnormal sleeping pattern. Sit up instead of lying down (unless you're trying to sleep of course; also, try to avoid multiple/daytime "naps"). Look out the window and focus on things in the distance if your eyes have been staring at a screen for hours. Drink lots (of water, not vodka). Keep your environment from looking like a nuclear bomb has hit.

Shower or bathe every day. Brush your teeth twice a day. Keep yourself dressed as much as possible. Eat a proper meal at the very least once every day. Snack less on things like crisps and sweets.

Try to eat a little better than you do, a little less sugar (unless you already eat really healthily and strictly, and then maybe don't be so hard on yourself all the time—reward yourself for moments of productivity).

It sometimes might feel like if you can't make a radical overhaul to your entire life then it's not worth it, that you either have to go big or give up before you've even begun. But that's just not true. I'm definitely an unhealthy eater, but I finally admitted to myself that I was having way too much sugar, and so my big grand diet was to eat one less dose of cake/cookies a day. That was it. And it was *hard*. Sometimes still is. I'm still unhealthy, and I'm still no doubt having too much sugar—but I'm that little bit better.

I'm trying to tell you that you can make tiny changes, and they all still count. They all still add up and make a difference. It's not a question of unhealthy, fat slob versus impossibly thin, perfect health freak. It's not a question of miserable, apathetic suicide-case or bouncing, happy-go-lucky flower child. Don't put your sights on the seemingly unattainable and think *ah fuck it, I'll never manage that*. Just make a few tiny changes, starting with the easiest. It's the same with exercise and anything else in your life that you feel you should change but it's all just too BIG to start. Stop seeing the forest; see the *trees*.

Regardless of what you do or don't eat, you should always aim to *enjoy* your food. This doesn't always happen (sometimes making meals can be such a chore, and the output can be less than inspiring), but you shouldn't give up on the pleasures of food entirely.

If you don't have food in your house, you MUST go and buy food. It doesn't have to be from a big, daunting grocery store, just the nearest place to get something quick to eat for the day.

These things might seem mind-numbingly regular—they are, and that's the point. When you're in a really bad state of mind, it's easy to slip up with these kinds of things. They can become harder and harder to do. *What's the point in keeping myself clean?* you might think. *It's effort, and I'm not even leaving the house where people can see me.*

You can see you. The Dark Side wants you to feel ugly and gross and empty inside and dehydrated and lethargic and miserable. It wants your room to look disgusting. It wants you off your meds. It wants you to lie in bed all day, it wants you unclean, it wants your hair oily, it wants you hungry, and it most *definitely* wants you to get acne. All these things just grease the wheels. They make it easier for it to pull you under.

Even when you don't want to do these things, *especially* when you don't, you have to keep the routine up. Get into the practice of bossing them. Perhaps that means a shower as the first thing when you get up every day. If you find yourself putting off just getting up for a drink of water, get yourself a really big glass or mug and keep it by you and sip it often.

I'm not saying that if you have a shower you'll bounce around, happy as sunshine. But everything involved in looking after yourself (and your immediate environment, which can easily influence your mood) are barriers and roadblocks: the defense mechanisms you need. They make it harder for okay to become bad, for bad to become worse, and for worse to become godawful.

Now get that lightsaber up and get in the shower.

A big part of the above suggestion for fighting the Dark Side might be:

POWER-UPS (aka MEDICATION)

Clinical depression isn't just "being sad." Clinical depression is an illness. Illnesses get treated. Chemical imbalances get better balanced. How can you process your problems when the very tool you are using to understand them with is fucked? A thing cannot reliably judge itself.

I might lose a few of my readers here. Of course not everyone needs to take any medicine, a great deal of you reading this won't. But those who do shouldn't avoid it like it's the bogeyman. If you can keep a good handle on your depression, anxiety, and suicidal feelings and they're not ruining your life and robbing you of control, then you can skim the rest of this section. Just be honest with yourself.

Give different types of medication a real chance. Try to avoid quackery. Follow doctor's orders (but make sure you ask them questions if you're unsure about something). And don't expect instant miracles. Misdiagnosis exists, unsympathetic doctors exist, and unpleasant side effects exist. Medication isn't always effective for particular people, some meds will trump others, it's never the be-all-end-all, and the field is ever learning and evolving. What can be perfect when it comes to people? Come to a gradual understanding between you and your chosen doctor (you don't have to stick with the same one) of what works for you and what doesn't. It's not a matter of go big or go broke. It's helping yourself in any small way you can. What makes you feel better? What makes life easier? What makes you a better person?

Don't fall into the trap of thinking that medication is a pointed statement that there's something intrinsically "wrong" with you. *Why should I change myself to fit the world, when it's the world that's awful and should be the one to change?* you might think. You see the sheer unfairness of it all. But it's not like that. It's adaptation. We adapt to fit the world in so many ways. Here are other things you could say in the same vein:

Why should I put on clothes to go outside? It's not my fault my body doesn't change its temperature enough to compensate, or that other people seem to have a problem with me being naked. Clothes aren't natural!

Why should I exercise? When do I get to stop exercising? What do you mean never?!

Why should I eat? My body should be self-sustaining. And you expect me to buy food? I didn't ask for this!

Imagine if Gandalf or Dumbledore came to you and told you that if you drank from this little purple vial once a day (and said the magic words), and kept on doing it, you could become a more productive, more efficient, less troubled, and altogether stronger, saner, calmer human being. Would you take it? And between you and me, I trust the average doctor a bit more than Gandalf and Dumbledore, given the shit they tried to pull.

Don't think of them as meds. Think of them as power-ups.

SUPPORT

There's no shame in asking for help. Everyone gets support, even if it's not always obvious. People get support from friends and family, from partners, from business associates, from bosses and from clients, from networking, from inheritance, from charities, from support groups, from online; many of the biggest, most powerful and influential people in the world have therapists—hell, their *therapists* have therapists.

Therapists, psychiatrists, clinical psychologists, doctors, and mental health nurses—they're all infinitely more trained and experienced than I am in these fields. Sure, not every single one can help you. They are people just like you and me after all. But a friendly ear is out there. Don't let one bad experience keep you from seeking professional support for the things you find toughest.

Asking for help isn't weak. It's not weakness to add another pillar under a building to better support the structure. It's simply good sense.

You've been fighting this whole time. Sometimes all you need is somebody to give you a bigger stick (or a triple-barreled shotgun, or a cat that shoots fireballs).

MOVIES

Be careful with your choice in movies. Don't watch romantic dramas or emotional rom-coms if you're really lonely and don't have anybody.

You have three good choices here: comfort watching, scary horror, and good comedy.

I haven't seen the movie *Misery* but I expect it's a close-up of my face for 2 hours

Comfort watching, the idea introduced to me by a friend, is watching something you already know and love, one of your old favorites. It should be something undemanding that you don't have to really concentrate on.

As for horror, I'm recommending this *especially* for people who don't normally watch horror. You see, fear is effective. It will rouse you from your stupor; it will make you feel where other things have failed to. You need to feel. It will also subtly activate your survival instinct, thus making you less likely to kill yourself right then. Or something like that. Sure, trembling wide-eyed in bed because you're scared stiff of the dark (and particularly what might be hiding in your cupboard or pressed up against the window, just waiting for you to open those curtains) might not be a particularly pleasant experience. But I bet it does more than most things to shake you out of your stupor.

But watch *entertaining* horror—I mean, don't watch something horrifically grim and relentlessly depressing. For the love of God, don't watch *Martyrs*.

When it comes to comedy, it's a bit risky in that there's a good chance it won't be funny to you. It's better not to take a chance on something new (unless you really think it's gonna be genuinely funny—good reviews and word-of-mouth, funny trailers) and stick to comfort watching. It's okay if watching a comedy doesn't make you laugh once. It doesn't necessarily mean the film is shit, and neither does it mean you're broken inside. You don't have to laugh. As long as it makes you feel a bit better watching it, a little bit warmer inside (or even just dams the flow of negativity, temporarily blocking it from making you any worse). You can find something pretty funny on the inside, without actually making any outward, physical acknowledgement of that fact.

I've lied, there's a fourth choice. I said don't watch emotional rom-coms if you don't have anybody (or if you have somebody who isn't perfect, which covers everybody else in the world). But there *is* something to be said for watching something that can make you blub. There are lots of good films out there with really heartfelt emotion-wringing moments. Crying is cathartic, especially when you have difficulty accessing genuine feelings. Sometimes it's hard to gather and express real, genuine emotions about ourselves and our lives (no matter how awful we may feel). We might need a little prompt, a push, a fiction to invest ourselves in, to make it

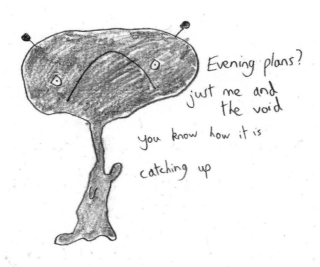

Evening plans?
just me and
the void
you know how it is
catching up

easier. There's a little tap inside you, and experiencing the right kind of moment (a movie, a piece of music, a book, maybe nothing at all) can give that squeaky rusting thing a jig, give it a good turn.

Maybe the crying happens because the film is making you think about yourself or your life in some way (as long as it's not the kind of thing that actually makes you feel worse about it all). Maybe in a particular character or situation you can find something to really relate to, things you really needed to hear somebody else say, things you really needed to see somebody else go through. Maybe it's an almost happy kind of crying. Maybe you're in tears simply because you're so wrapped up in the story and the characters and what's happening at that particular moment in the movie. Whatever the reasons, it's good. It's not crying for no reason, crying for crying's sake. It's not crying out of emptiness. It's turning the tap and bringing out these real feelings, these completely human emotions out of the numbness.

The kind of emotional movies to watch are ones that a) never fail to make you weepy, and b) aren't depressing, perhaps not even truly sad. You know what I mean? Where you cry but you aren't *upset*. An otherwise lovely, maybe even uplifting and funny movie, but nonetheless a sentimental one that has a tendency to wring the emotions. Certainly not a depressing-sad movie. There can be a thin line at times, but you'll know best.

Watch them alone, or with somebody you aren't in the slightest bit awkward to let loose around.

My recommendations (fully aware that you might think they're a load of crap) to readers of this book, you imaginative pessimists, you self-destructive psychonauts:

Mary and Max, *The Fall* (2006), *Eternal Sunshine of the Spotless Mind*, *Inside Out*, *Into the Wild*, *Swiss Army Man*, *A Beautiful Mind*, *The Little Prince* (2015), *Groundhog Day*, *Life is Beautiful*, *Hugo*, *It's a Wonderful Life*, *Modern Times*, *Pink Floyd: The Wall*, *Her*, *Dead Man*, *Pan's Labyrinth*, *A Monster Calls*, *Quills*, *The Aviator*, *Waking Life*, *Earth* (2007 nature documentary based on the BBC Attenborough series *Planet Earth*—watch to help you believe again that there's beauty in the world; in fact, watch all the various BBC natural history Attenborough series, I'm sure you won't regret it), and *Schindler's List* (yeah, I know, but it's about saving lives).

I'm tempted to add *Melancholia* to my suggestions, as it paints such a horribly accurate picture of extreme depression, but you're probably more likely to want to kill yourself after watching it, which I think we're trying to avoid.

Oh, and *Jurassic Park*. Not for any relevant reason. Just because dinosaurs.

HELP OTHER PEOPLE

"No one is useless in this world who lightens the burden of it for anyone else." –Charles Dickens

Helping other people will help you help yourself. You know it's true. It takes you away from your own problems and makes you concentrate on someone else for a change. It makes you feel worthwhile and wanted (even *liked*). It shows that other people need help and support just like you (whether they admit it or not—almost nobody is as happy as they seem). And it puts your problems in perspective. Either because somebody else's problems seem so much worse, or because their problems are so ridiculously petty and inane that a) you can give them advice pretty easily and act the super-wise village elder, b) it proves your strength handling your own problems, given that other people seem to fall apart so easily in comparison, or/and c) you find their problems rather funny (best keep this to yourself).

The best reason though, is that helping people with issues that correlate with yours actually helps you deal with your own, precisely because, without realizing it at first, you're giving *yourself* advice. You're just speaking it out loud, working through it with another person under the guise of helping them.

Realize what you're saying. Recognize and understand what you observe in this other person and the behaviors you find unpleasant, damaging, and off-putting to others that are echoed within yourself. Notice the complaints and defensive arguments you see as stupid and irrational and easily countered. It's all so obvious isn't it? Why don't they just *listen* to you?

Listen to yourself. Try to take your own advice. Kill two birds with one stone.

Oh, but also take care to . . .

AVOID OTHER PEOPLE

Recognize and then limit the amount of time you spend with negative people in your life. I'm not saying don't keep them as your friends (though you should know when it's time to truly let them go, when they are simply not a good friend to you by any means). You can still help them, if they need you to (although it should go both ways; they should also be there for *you*), but you only have so much to give. You have to look after yourself, too. You have your own problems.

Too much negativity—whether it's about their own problems or, worse, about you and yours—can drain you and even devastate your own sense of self-worth. They can shut down happy thoughts before they're even allowed to surface.

Negative people do deserve friends, and they deserve attention and support. After all, you're one! But they should never dominate somebody's life, nor should they drain it for themselves. Try to spend time with positive people as well. Or middle-ground people—those who see that the glass is half empty, but still appreciate the drink that's in it. They're the best.

There's only one type of person better to spend company with. And that's yourself.

Oh, and try avoid spending too much time being a digital masochist and engaging with hateful, obnoxious, and grossly ignorant people online. You know neither side will ever convince the other—all you're doing is frustrating yourself, and probably encouraging them. Social media can be a hive of scum and villainy. Stay in the light if you can.

ARGUE WITH YOUR BAD THOUGHTS

You know you overthink. You know your mind takes you down some pretty dark paths. Are these thoughts thoroughly justified? Are you sure?

Here's the deal. Have you seen many courtroom dramas? You're a lawyer, best in the land (Yes, you are. Because I say so). Everyone's tense, everyone's holding their breath. You've won every trial you've ever been part of. You can't afford to slip up now, you have a reputation to uphold. But this, this is the hardest trial you've ever had to face, and it just keeps going. Day after day you're back in the courtroom. You have to win. Everybody is counting on it, not least yourself. Everything rests on proving the accused wrong.

The person in the hot seat? Yourself. You're prosecuting yourself.

Should that mean you give up, that it's unwinnable? Of course not. That person in the chair might be you, but that doesn't mean you can't beat them. If anything, you're the best person to beat them. Look at their glum fucking face. Did they just bite a lemon? You can take them. You have logic and rationality on your side. And they—well, they're full of shit! Can't the jury see that? Can't *you* see that?

Unfortunately not. That's why you gotta step up your game. You have to dismantle everything that comes out of that person's mouth.

Hello darkness
my old friend
well
more like
an acquaintance

Open up your suitcase, get out those case notes. It's time to get to work.

Here's what you do. When you can't sleep, when you're depressed, or down, or anxious, or whatever (but not so horrifically bad that you can't even pick up a pen), get some paper and write down, on the left-hand side, all the awful things you're thinking—about yourself, about the world, about other people, about your future. All of it. Especially about the future. Try to write down reasons to think this way. Bullet-point it if you think you'll end up writing an essay otherwise.

Now you're on the offensive. Super-lawyer mode. You are going to pick apart every single one of these ideas and assertions. On the right-hand side of the paper you should do your damnedest to think of all the sensible reasons and evidence you can that challenge and oppose each thing on the left-hand side.

It doesn't matter if you don't really believe in your argument at that moment. You're a lawyer, who cares about what you believe! Just come up with the damn case! Even if you have to call on character witnesses (every good lawyer needs other people to support their case). Screw stray emotions. You're using logic and reason and pure hard-nosed argument now. Win.

Whenever you think the same awful things again, look back at that paper and read it. If you come up with new things to worry about, get another piece of paper.

Keep these lists by your bed.

For a simpler, stripped down offshoot of the whole courtroom tactic, combat stray irrational, super-negative thoughts like you're playing tennis. Either against a ball machine or another person—an evil, shadow-person. Each ball is a negative thought that has no practical purpose. Its intent is to get you to dwell on it, for no other reason than to waste your time and get you down.

Thwack those thoughts back every time. BAM! *Right back atcha.*

Then immediately try to shift your thoughts to something else. Perhaps what you were thinking about before that big black ball was smacked at you. Occupy yourself. Distract yourself.

Didn't work? The ball came back? Of course it did! Who said this tennis was a one-hit-and-you're-done affair? Hit it back again! BAM!

The best players have had the longest practices.

THERE'S A LIST YOU SHOULD MAKE. RIGHT NOW.

Go on, get some paper and a pen. Or write it on your phone, if you're always glued to it.

The list is called "Straightforward Reasons To Stay Alive," or "Simple Reasons to Stay Alive," and it's exactly that. What you are going to do is write down a whole load of reasons to stay alive, and you are going to look at it whenever you really need to. This list will be full of straightforward and simple things. By that, I mean you are not writing down anything that has the potential to fill you full of doubts, anything up in the air, anything that includes uncertainty or mixed feelings, and certainly not anything complex. You want things your depressed mind is least likely to dismiss.

You are not to write in a general way about friends or family or partners (you might write about pets, though). You are not to write about careers. You are not even to write about your creative or worldly ambitions. These are hopes and ideals, and they are anything but straightforward.

No, what you need when you are feeling suicidal is stability. Concrete things you know you can rely on. Immediate comforts. Things to look forward to. Things that don't just go away. Things that still have the ability to give you pleasure, or if you're beyond pleasure, at least some measure of satisfaction. And you shouldn't worry a damn about how materialistic the list might seem, especially if it seems really silly or trite. This is about the simple things.

It is a list of things you like that you will miss out on if you die. And it might just be the little barrier you need that will keep you away from that ledge.

The best way I can explain what I mean is to give you my own list. Don't judge me . . .

SET'S SIMPLE (AND SFW) REASONS TO STAY ALIVE (in no particular order)

- Cheese
- Cake
- Everything that cheese and cake go with

- Upcoming superhero movies

- Future LEGO video games

- Future *Assassin's Creed* games

- Future albums by bands I really like (like Those Poor Bastards)

- Everything and anything Batman, in the past, present, and especially the future

- Future seasons of the show *Gotham* (if it's cancelled by the time you read this, then I'm COMING FOR *YOU!*)

- Acquiring all the books, graphic novels/comics, DVDs, albums, clothes and weird miscellaneous items on my 20-pages-and-only-ever-growing "Things I Want" list

- Going back to Disney World & Universal Studios in Florida (my favorite place)

- The smell in green areas after it rains

- Deep forests and little winding streams

- Warm sunshine and blue skies

- Tropical sights of beaches and palm trees (even if it's just computer wallpaper)

- Neon signs at night

- Cuddly animals (including ones that would kill me if I ever tried to cuddle them)

- Long, hot showers (that don't suddenly go freezing/boiling for absolutely no reason)

- Incredible music and movies and shows and games and books that just blow me away/make me melt inside

- A particular example to mention is the show *Gravity Falls* (not the individual episodes, but the thing as a whole, or rather, the state in which it exists in my mind, its world—oh, and that theme tune!) and that indescribable warm feeling I get whenever I think about it all, as though I'm party to some kind of strange and almost hauntingly magical atmosphere that I can't help but be enlivened and inspired by; in short, like a number of things, it's not about what it *is* so much as what it represents to me, and what my mind can do with it

- Singing along to songs (especially '50s rock 'n' roll) when nobody else is around to judge me, and feeling like I'm completely in tune (regardless of the reality)

- Looking at my book collection (just looking at it, picking books up and flicking through and putting them back and picking up another . . . maybe smelling a few . . .)

- The small sense of pride and warm satisfaction from a successful writing session, where I can read it back and think, *Hey, I can write!*

- The even greater sense of pride and satisfaction from finishing a whole novel and reading it back, and knowing that *I did it*—from beginning to end it was all me, and for a little while I feel like a productive and useful human being

And so on. You get the picture. These are all things that give me some not insignificant measure of joy and satisfaction and which I don't want to miss out on. Case in point is the show *Gotham*. I'm writing this in 2016-17, and Season 3 is currently airing (I'm telling you this in case it all goes to shit later on). I don't care what you think of the show (nor should you care when it comes to your own precious entertainments), it's enough that I am completely invested in future seasons. Hell, even when I'm watching the *current* season I can't wait for the next season. I get excited—or whatever passes for excitement when it comes to me—when a new season draws near. I look up everything there is to do with it. And—this will sound pretty sad and weird—I look forward to seeing the young actor David Mazouz naturally age season by season, bit by bit growing into an adult Bruce Wayne. Dammit, I want to see what he looks like in 2 years, in 5, in 10! You better be working out, David! Put on that muscle! LIFT!

Gotham is also an ideal choice for the list because it's not a flash-in-the-pan thing. There's a good chance it'll keep going for many seasons (it bloody better). The longer it lasts, the better for me.

Gotham keeps me looking forward.

ESCAPE

If something is causing you very direct, very immediate and noticeable frustration, **escape the situation**. Do not let it fester. Do not just wait it out.

For example, if you're frustrated by being in a particular room with someone, like a partner or family member, then leave the room. If you're having an especially difficult and unpleasant conversation with someone, end the conversation (politely if at all possible). Make some excuse (or tell the truth) and leave the room if necessary. If things on the internet are pissing you off, exit your browser (and maybe turn off the internet for a while). Unfollow things and people on Facebook that consistently wind you up—you really won't miss them.

You can also escape from something bad by escaping to something good. Movies. Shows. Games. Books. Comics. Music. Art and entertainment of any kind. Or there's nature to enjoy and lose yourself in (admittedly that's in the big scary Outside). Or just create your own world, your own reality. Imagine. Invent.

Don't let anybody tell you that escapism is inherently something bad. That you should be "living in the Real World." Fuck those people. Okay, so maybe some of them are still decent people, and you like them, so you just want to ignore some of the things they say.

What we call escapism is part and parcel of the human existence. It is part of the reality we live in, and it is essential for people like us, and a great many people not like us too.

Finally, following on from the last point, and this is important:

MAKE SURE ANYBODY WHO LIVES WITH YOU (OR SOMEONE CLOSE WHO YOU SPEND A LOT OF TIME WITH) KNOWS ABOUT YOUR DEPRESSION

You don't have to tell them everything (although if you trust them, and they're good to you, do so). But you don't want to alienate family, friends, and partners—that will make things worse. You need them to understand that sometimes you just need to leave the room, for example. Try to explain the signs to them (imagine yourself in their shoes looking at you in one of your moods), and apologize in advance for how you'll be, but that it's nothing personal (even if, during the mood, it may seem really personal).

This will make things easier, and hopefully remove or lessen potential sources of frustration.

For example, I might explain (when I'm in a warmer mood) the following points:

- *If there's a time where I'm barely responding, I'm sullen and grouchy, and my face looks completely lifeless or like I've swallowed a lemon, then don't try to engage me too much. Try to recognize these kinds of cues and their repetitions, their similarities to previous times. Try to remember what worked better than other things. Leave me in my own company, but check in every so often, such as every half hour or hour. Just busy yourself doing your own thing, but perhaps have very short undemanding exchanges with me. This will keep me from thinking you're in a mood with me, which would only encourage my own mood. But neither will it frustrate me by expecting too much of me.*

- *Let me listen to my music or watch my things relatively undisturbed. If I seem pissed off that you're interrupting anything, don't interrupt any more—but still make your presence seen every so often; don't just leave me to stew for hours at a time or I'll imagine that you hate me and have given up on me. I don't hate you, no matter how I act around you. I'm just cold and numb and dark inside. Don't take anything personally.*

- *Don't badger me, don't shout or go on and on about things, don't pick that time to complain (unless you're sharing my own complaints). Don't aggressively try to make me feel better or pick through my problems with a fine-toothed comb. And don't try to hug or kiss me—the thought is appreciated, but it might feel really invasive; yes, you know I care about you and I like your affection, but right then in that mood of mine you may as well just pour a tub of spiders down my back.*

- *Ask me how I am. Not all the time, but don't just do it once at the start then give up. Of course I'm going to give you a shit answer. But it might be a springboard into me speaking more. Accept that my talk might be thoroughly dark and depressing. It's a good sign that I'm speaking in full sentences. Talking to me, even in short bursts, and asking me how I am or if there's anything particular upsetting me at the moment, might be all I need to open up. I might really, desperately want to clear the air, especially if we've fallen out (or maybe I just think we have). I won't be the first one to make the effort. I'll just stew, and make things worse in my mind. I'm sorry, but I need you to be the one to start. Every time.*

- *It might be horrible to begin with, but it'll get easier. You might not think you've made any headway, but providing you weren't confrontational or judgmental, and you showed no sign of frustration or anger with me, then you have. It doesn't matter if my voice is still a monotone and I haven't said anything even remotely positive in hours. You've helped.*

- *When I'm at least talking, and seem like I have enough energy to do difficult things like stand up and sit down, suggest playing a game with me or watching something, or (God forbid) even a walk. Keeping me company without placing any demands on me can definitely help at certain times. We don't even have to be doing the same thing; sometimes it's just nice to have someone in the same room, even if we're both on our phones or laptops and saying next to nothing. There's no real pressure to be sociable, I'm not feeling particularly judged, nobody's giving me a hard time. You're just letting me be miserable, but you're also still there, you still welcome my company—and that means everything. You're telling me, without speaking: I know you're completely depressed, but I still like you.*

- *Try to learn from every episode, and I will too—never just assume you can't ever help, but recognize the times when I'm better off being given space for a while.*

- *Talk to me about it when I'm feeling a bit better. Ask me what you did that made it worse and what you did that made it a bit better. Accept that you won't always be able to help (sometimes it might seem like anything you do or say is a total waste of time), and I'm not just a problem you can "fix" in the moment, but that's okay. It's about more than that, and the support and help you've given me isn't always clear and visible—but that doesn't mean it's not there.*

- *And thank you. Thank you for trying, whether it worked or not. Thank you for being there.*

Some of these suggestions won't apply to you, or just won't work the same way. Try to recognize your own behaviors, especially when they occur frequently, or if they always have the same catalysts (particularly if the things that set you off are preventable). Understand what makes you feel worse, and what makes you feel a little bit more comfortable. You need to fully recognize these things yourself if you have any hope of explaining them patiently and calmly to others.

If they don't have much of a clue, ask them to research depression and other issues online. Show them links you've found yourself (there's some at the end of this book) that you believe explain what you're going through better than most (insightful webcomic strips are good, seeing as most people aren't about to read a proper article). Direct them to challenge their own bad assumptions.

Make sure they know that the following phrases are not only incredibly unhelpful, but can actually make things worse:

- Cheer up.

- Turn that frown upside down.

- People starving in Africa have it worse than you.

- You should try to think happy thoughts.

- Stop being in a mood.

- There's nothing wrong with you (wait, did I tell you that earlier? Erm . . . *runs away*).

- Get over it.

- You should try this (insert bullshit remedy/ old wives' tale/something to do with positive energy), it made me feel great.

- You're just being a Negative Nancy.

If they don't understand, no matter how much you try to explain, if they don't even try to better understand, fuck 'em. They're not good for you.

DREAM THE BEST BE THE BEST

"Life is not an easy matter . . . You cannot live through it without falling into frustration and cynicism unless you have before you a great idea which raises you above personal misery, above weakness, above all kinds of perfidy and baseness." —Leon Trotsky

When people talk about Maslow's classic Hierarchy of Needs, they are usually referring to the lower tiers: physiological needs, safety needs, needs of companionship and affection, etc. But at the top of this hierarchy is self-actualization, appearing even above esteem needs (although it can be heavily tied to self-esteem). Self-actualization can include, in various models of this hierarchy, cognitive needs (a search for knowledge and meaning), aesthetic needs (a quest for beauty), self-fulfillment, seeking personal growth, transcendence needs (helping others to self-actualize), and "peak experiences."

Maslow identified fifteen characteristics of a self-actualized person, together with a list of behavior leading to self-actualization. I *was* about to just go and just dump them all here, but our lawyer-king Joe tells me (from his throne made from the tears of writers—no, no, he's actually lovely . . . they're tears of joy . . . *don't hurt me Joe!*) that I can't just go copying whole great bunches of content willy-nilly. So I'm just going to close my eyes and remember/imagine what the list probably contained. I reckon it'll be close enough.

Okay, so I'll just open my eyes a tiny fraction. So I can see the keyboard.

Characteristics of self-actualizers (as transcribed from memory by me):

1. They know what reality is (even if they don't like it). Um.

2. They know they're different but they accept that, more or less. Except perhaps when people stare at them on the bus.

3. They like to do things without thinking them through. Some call it spontaneity. Others try to get you institutionalized.

4. Pillow forts.

5. They have the sort of sense of humor that makes people worry about them sometimes.

6. Inanimate objects *might* have feelings. You never know.

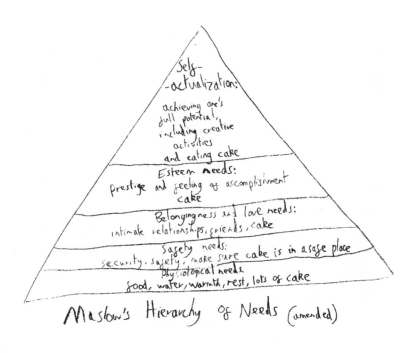

Self-actualization:
achieving one's
full potential,
including creative
activities
and eating cake

Esteem needs:
prestige and feeling of accomplishment
cake

Belongingness and love needs:
intimate relationships, friends, cake

Safety needs:
security, safety, make sure cake is in a safe place

Physiological needs
food, water, warmth, rest, lots of cake

Maslow's Hierarchy of Needs (amended)

7. Super creative and all that.

8. They neither go along with the crowd, nor do they deliberately try to be weirdos—it just comes naturally.

9. They care about humanity. Sort of. Sometimes. I mean, I guess it depends how much time you spend on social media.

10. Ten . . . number ten . . . er, they usually like really soft cuddly things?

11. They like to have deeper, more personal relationships with a few people rather than more superficial relationships with lots of people. Could also be phrased as "doesn't have many friends."

12. Peak experiences. Erm, how do I describe this . . . Okay, basically, you know when you have one of those fruit lollies in their own packaging—I think in America you might call them freezie pops? Anyway, you take one of these particularly tasty Freedom Pops and you don't lick it, you just let it melt, crushing the packaging every so often to speed the process up (because patience is for the weak). When it's close enough to fully melted, you put it to your mouth, tip your head back and drink that sweet, sweet nectar. That's a peak experience.

13. They really need privacy (I call it recharge time—being around people drains my batteries). They might even have that polite "leave me the fuck alone" face.

15. They have pretty strong morals and ethics. Unless someone gives them a sword or a big stick to hold.

15. Cake. Cake is nice. What is this list about again?

Behavior leading to self-actualization:

(a) You're basically a child wearing an adult skin.

(b) You prefer to try new things rather than being a Boring Brian (truly sorry if that's actually your name—forge your own path Brian, don't let your name define you!).

(c) You prefer to listen to your own feelings and inner voice in judging situations for yourself rather than what the majority, authorities, or good ol' tradition have to say about them.

(d) You prefer to be honest and true with people rather than messing about like a total donk (which wastes *everybody's* time— yes, I'm looking at you Game-Playing Gertrude and Messing-About Michael!)

(e) Putting random objects on your own/other people's heads and declaring "it's a hat."

(f) Identifying your own inner defenses and being brave enough to take them down in order to better yourself.

(g) Being prepared to be unpopular when you put yourself in the minority by your own behavior, actions or attitudes. Continuing as you are anyway because staying true to yourself is more important than being popular.

Of course, there will be a number of these points that you don't relate to one bit. Me too. People becoming self-actualized (bearing in mind it's kind of a journey without actual end, like exercising) all do it in their own unique way, but they often enough share characteristics.

Take note of a few, slightly surprising ones. Being like a child in at least some ways. Having the courage to give up your own defenses. Being prepared to be unpopular when you put yourself in the minority (imaginative pessimists are always in the minority, and we feel it very keenly). Listening to your own feelings instead of the voice of others. Need for privacy. Resistant to "fitting in," but not on purpose. Unusual sense of humor. Spontaneous.

And, of course, highly creative.

How interesting. You thought it was a curse, didn't you? Unfitting for the Real World, something that often seems to actively hold you back? Your whole life you've felt like you belong to a different time and place, maybe even to a different species. Your skills and passions have seemed entirely non-transferable to the fields of ordinary work—and even when in a supposedly creative job, your passion has been boxed in and checked off. "Draw between the lines," life has commanded you from the moment you were born. *Always* draw between the lines.

The regular 9 to 5 has been anathema to you. Your mind drifts away at every possible pause for breath, desperate to be away from the organized monotony, the rules and regulations, the menial tasks—none of which mean the slightest thing to you. What is the point in them, when it'll be the same again the next day, and the day after? What is the *point*? Life seems to be nothing other than living out the tale of Sisyphus, rolling that boulder up the hill again and again. And yet other people, despite their common and consistent complaining, seem content to live the rat race. It's just "one of those things," isn't it?

Get a career. Work hard. Make money. Get promoted. Make more money. Settle down. Get job security. Get life security. Forget your dreams, your imagination—it's of no use here. Focus, stay grounded, keep yourself busy, don't think too much. Live in the Real World. Box yourself in. Keep yourself drawn between the lines. And don't forget about your pension!

The thought of curtailing this bubbling pot inside yourself, a life of keeping the lid on, shutting it up, just keep working, just keep working . . . The thought fills you with unimaginable horror and despair. It's not just horrible and soulless, it might even be *impossible*.

Your mind floats, flies . . . and then is brought back to earth as your boss shouts at you, recognizing that away-with-the-fairies look in your eyes. Down we go. Bump.

A curse, huh? It's easy to think of it in that way, because we're so used to living life in a very particular, specified way. We've grown up, been schooled, and been talked down to all the same from the very beginning, always to do it one way, to think of yourself and how useful you can be to society by the narrowest of understanding. It's incredibly hard to shake that—and society is very resistant to losing its chokehold on you. The machine wants every man, woman, and child it can get.

It's one thing if you like your chosen career, if you have something you're good at and can excel at, something that makes you feel useful and valued to some degree and doesn't crush your spirit. Or perhaps you recognize work can be merely tolerated, a necessary evil, and you get value out of life from everything outside of work. For those types, all the more power to you. But if you're not built that way . . . well, you may as well put a hamster in a square wheel. Sometimes tasks so simple and straightforward to other people are really bloody difficult when your mind just doesn't organize itself that way. You can't always expect somebody who is busy thinking about how to design a floating castle to also be much good at making sandwiches.

It's not a curse. Yeah, it can be tough as nails, and yeah, there's a hell of a lot out there it just won't gel with. You'll struggle more than most. But that doesn't mean you can't still come out on top, and that the sky won't be brighter and the air so much cleaner when you do. And it sure doesn't mean you can't value yourself and admire yourself. Be *proud* of yourself.

Remember, being highly creative is a key part of being a self-actualized person—the highest rung of what somebody needs out of life. You don't have to be a painter or a writer to be creative. It might just be in the crazy workings of your mind, and the way you see the world.

Don't let it go. Don't hate it. Don't consider it a weakness. It's not a curse. It's fucking amazing.

Fitting a triangle into a square-shaped hole doesn't work too well, and it'll be very frustrating to try. But just wait until you find that triangle-shaped hole.

I am a potato

IMMORTALITY

"I have immortal longings in me."

—Shakespeare, *Antony and Cleopatra*

Our ability to create, invent, and imagine is what separates us from other animals. If you are really creative and imaginative then you possess one of the most highly valued qualities conceivable in abundance.

You could say that that makes you better than people who aren't creative. More prone to depression, despair, and disillusionment than they are, perhaps, but nonetheless better.

Let me back that up.

You hold on to these "escapisms"—fictions, inventions, creations— as either your raison d'etre or, for the pessimist's mind, your "reason for not dying yet," aka "what has kept me going so far." You might even think, whether in vague and idealistic or very real terms, that these creations (books, games, paintings, movies, music, television series) have in some way saved your life.

They inspire you, not just for your own creativity, but they inspire you to see the world and your own existence—and other people's existence—in a new light. They inspire you to smile, to laugh, to cry, to wonder, to think. They make you dream. They distract you from mundanity and depression, or they convert it, at least for a spell (and a spell is what it is), into something better.

Not just that, but they inspire you because of the sheer power it took to create them. Physical manifestations coming from the absurd, wondrous, magical, transcendent, insane minds of humans. Maybe humans just like you. Maybe kindred souls. Maybe you're not alone.

Yes, you have that power too. It may be dormant within you, or maybe you are pulling and tugging at it already, but I'm willing to bet you don't see it for what it truly is, that you would never dare (except with a shiver of self-consciousness and shame) give your name in the same breath as the masterly inspirations you treasure most wildly.

You're *not* alone, and you have a great deal in common with the people behind the works that saved your life, whether it was directly or indirectly. Most creative types were imaginative pessimists for a time, if not forever. They struggled with life, just like you. The tortured artist is a well-known stereotype for a reason.

These people that you look up to, that (especially if they are long dead) seem distant and otherworldly, half-fictional in themselves, they were very real people who wept and suffered, who doubtless often hated themselves and the world around them, and many of them would have had suicidal thoughts (and some even went all the way, and were celebrated posthumously). They would have doubted themselves, doubted ten thousand leagues beyond doubt; they would have thought they were nothing, that their work was terrible, and they would never dare (except with a shiver of self-consciousness and shame) give their name in the same breath as the masterly inspirations they treasured most wildly.

Half-fictional, I said. Well perhaps they are now—their works were fictions, and they are known far more for them than they were for their personalities . . . and in the end, what you are remembered for becomes you, and you are just another character, and your works are fictions of fictions. This is not a bad thing. This is an amazing thing, something of near perfection. People don't last, but fiction does. Art does. We are fragile and mortal; we get ugly, we fall sick, and we die. Beautiful paintings, beautiful music, beautiful books, and beautiful characters stay beautiful. They remain as intense and burning as they were when they were first made. Nothing gets old. The characters of these great people are remembered, and they become timeless. They will never die.

A thousand years from now, people will find your work and they will absorb it, will drink it in, and it will be like you are in the room with them. You will have crossed boundaries of space and time, crossed death itself, and reached out to them. You have made an impact. You have made a difference.

What other professions and pursuits can say the same? Sure, you can make a difference to one generation, and so by affecting the lives of grandparents you in turn affect the lives of parents, and so then the children. But by the time it gets to the grandchildren, it's a thoroughly indirect difference, not keenly felt, if felt at all. Whereas art has an immediate, direct connection, a hotline straight to a person's heart and soul, no matter how distant and alien they might be to you, no matter what far-flung time or place.

They will know you for who you are.

YOU CAN BE MORE

There's something you need to consider, and it is one of the most important things I can tell you. You are—or can be—*other people's reason for living.* People you've never met, people you've never even seen or heard of. They need you. They need what you can give them. They need your creations.

Imaginative pessimists are artists (even if you have not started yet, or found your chosen discipline). Whether it is writing, drawing, painting, filming, sculpting, crafting, sewing, building, cooking, photography, photo manipulation, animation, programming, game design, graphic design, fashion design, architectural design, landscape design, acting, dancing, making movies, making music, making people laugh, or whatever else. What you are doing, or could be doing, is *extraordinary.* It takes a god to create something from nothing (or from very little, something intangible, an idea, the merest flitting of inspiration).

Am I calling you a god? Yes, yes I am.

Is that quite ridiculous? Yes it is, we both know that. But whether you believe it or not (most likely you don't—we were raised to be many things, but not fools) I want you to pretend to believe it, or half-believe it in a deep, secret part of you. I want you to go along with it, like it's a joke we're both in on. Don't tell anyone else, this is something just for you. Also, they'll either think you a complete narcissist or completely crazy, or both.

Why should you foster this idea in yourself? It's easy. One word, and it's central to this entire guide. I've already brought it up once, but now it's time to put it through the wringer.

EGO

Your ego is vital to your survival. It's common to go through life imagining the ego as a bad thing; after all it's most often seen in the form of "egotistical," which is always presented as something bad.

It can be bad, if you're being arrogant to others or if you show a lack of care and respect as to how you deal with others. But ego is also, when controlled, what gives you confidence—with others as with yourself. It's what gives you pride in yourself and your creations. To survive, you must put yourself at least on the same pedestal as those around you.

Not all, but a lot of suicidal people are egotistical. I don't say this as a bad thing. Egotism has two distinct forms. There's the

Hobbies?
Does lying
face down
on the
floor
count

belief that you are great, brilliant, and amazing as you are. This is the bad kind of egotism. Then there is the belief that you *can be* great, brilliant, and amazing as *you have the potential to be*. This is the good, life-enriching kind of egotism. This latter belief will always be striving for more, tempered as it is with its own modest, skeptical sense of reality (unlike the former kind, which lurches out unchecked, resting on the dangerous and distasteful assumption that *I can do no wrong*).

Imaginative pessimists are more likely to possess the latter kind of egotism, the restless, crystal-ball-gazing kind, and it is this latter idea that I wish to encourage within you. This sense of ego and narcissism correlates with the push towards suicidal impulses— because it is the expression of a desire for something more, and it is that which is getting repeatedly crushed by the Real World.

If you had a choice in any given situation to feel the following, which would you choose: to feel like you were worse than everybody else, or to feel you were better than everybody else?

Sure, you might ask for a middle ground—and certainly, that's a good course for life in general. But for these given situations, it should always be the second choice that you foster within—clandestinely, of course—don't make it too obvious. But if you nurture it, if you feed it, if you pretend so long that it becomes at least half-real, you will find yourself walking a new walk, talking a new talk, and carrying yourself as you ought to be carried.

I'm not too worried about letting the ego spin too far out of control. As long as you don't let it get too insular, to the point you can't relate to others and you end up further isolated and alienated. Keep an *open* ego, if that makes any sense whatsoever. Nobody likes an elitist!

If you get near the point of your ego becoming too strong and hard-bitten, I believe that a wise soul like you will know about it (or others will be sure to tell you). You've spent so much time in introspection, you've spent so much time feeling awful about yourself, feeling like you were nothing, that feelings of sudden empowerment and self-belief will be fiercely observed within you. You should—and I'm sure you will—take note of every little moment where you think to yourself, in a tiny little voice that your instincts tell you to suppress, to shush: right now I'm damn cool. It should have no bearing on your interactions with others (don't act like a dick, that's not what this is about at all), except they'll have a newfound respect and admiration for your confidence, and you in turn will feel happier to be around them, not feeling quite as squashed and useless as before.

That little voice won't be there all the time—and it never will be, not with people like us. You'll always be fighting off the low times—I'm not going to come out like a prophet and tell you that one day you'll be completely free of all this. But what I am saying is that you will get better, and that the damn cool times will come more often, at the expense of less hate-myself-hate-the-world times.

For hating yourself and hating the world go hand in hand. When you feel one, you inevitably feel the other, even if one takes precedence. When you feel inspired by yourself—whether it's by your own creative output, your own actions, hell, your own appearance—the world will seem that little bit brighter. You might even start smiling, and things will start to seem not so shitty anymore. Possibly even, y'know, kinda good (if you're anything like me, you might quickly counter this with "well, obviously things are still bloody crap in general, and I hate most things, but right now . . . well let's just forget about all that and enjoy the moment, yes?")

Life is all about enjoying the moments. The little things. That's one of those trite things, and I know I've railed against the trite things of self-help books earlier, but, well . . . I guess I'm a massive hypocrite. Roll with it.

CHANGE

"Our life is what our thoughts make it." –Marcus Aurelius

I f you feel better, the world will be better. Repeat that to yourself. Only change "you" to "I," or you'll look like you're anthropomorphizing whatever you're reading this on, which probably won't respond back.

Notice I said "will be" and not "will seem." I wrote "will seem" to begin with, and then I deleted it. The quality of the world is entirely subjective, and we all know that to be self-evident, and so the quality of the world, and the truth of statements like "today is all right" and "the world isn't full of shit" lie entirely in your own head. It is *you* who controls how good the world is or isn't, how bearable living here is, and nobody else. There could be a nuclear war that lays all the greenness of the land and all the beautiful animal life to waste, and afterwards some hermit will emerge from his bunker and say, "The world is actually all right today," and still be correct, just as right as he'd be if he'd said, "Oh, for fuck's sake."

And so, "will be" and "will seem" are the same thing. Therefore I chose "will be," because it is the first illustration of your powers as a god. What happens on the inside, you realize, happens on the outside.

Transmogrification! Your new power. Use it wisely.

With great power

comes

great

responsibility.

Your friend in need, your friend indeed,

Set Sytes

P.S. Make good on your ideas.

P.P.S. Keep on chooglin'. It gets better.

•   •   •

This is the most important quote I can give you. Remember it well, especially in the dead of night when all seems hopeless.

"This too shall pass."
—Proverb

A SELF-SERVING AFTERWORD

I like to write. I don't *love* to write, at least not always, but it's kind of the only thing I'm any good at. Writing can be painful, especially if my darker nature is informing it. What's more painful than writing, though, is writing and not being read.

Writing a story is like giving birth (certainly just as messy). A story is one of my children. I give it all the love and attention and care I can, but at a certain point it's no longer solely up to me. When the world neglects a story, they neglect my child. And it's horribly, terribly hard to let them go.

And so what do I do?

I get disillusioned, I get depressed. And then, inevitably, I "bounce back" in some small way (past wounds add to each other, clustering together) and I write more. I do that because it's the only thing I can do, and because there's still so much in me that begs to come out, that begs to be heard.

And, more than anything else, I do it because of my ego and my stubbornness.

I write more, and I write better.

My stories are ones of fantasy and horror, science fiction and dystopian and western. I like the dark and the weird (and, of course, the funny). I don't like anything commonplace and ordinary, nothing here-and-now-and-just-as-we-are. That doesn't mean the Real World doesn't inform and insert itself in all my stories. How we live, where we live, and who we live with are all as essential to otherworldly fiction as any other genre. The Real World and all its workings are the bones of fantasy. Even goblins and aliens feel. Even they have rules, whether they follow them or break them.

I have lived most of my adult life failing at it, while miraculously still being alive. I had the fortune and privilege of a great childhood, but when you're up that high you have even further to fall. The Real World was not interested in my imagination, in the things I so desperately wanted from the world. I always wanted more. I still do, and I always will.

The Real World told me, again and again, "What are you doing?! You're no good at this! You're hopeless!" and I would respond, again and again with, "I KNOW!!!"

once upon a time

every body died

The end

Writing saved me, and it's still saving me. It's got a lot of saving still to come.

I worry that this book won't be enough. That there will always be people I can't reach, people I can't help. The truth is that if this is read by ten thousand people and it miraculously helps save one person's life, then it has been entirely justified. That's what it's about. I just wish my head could always see it that way. I always want more.

Writing *How Not to Kill Yourself* was very different from writing stories. I feel more naked writing it. On display. I don't think there will ever come a time when I re-read it without finding some small part that makes me cringe. *Why did I write that?* I'll ask myself. *Did I think that was good advice? Was I trying to be funny? It doesn't even make sense. It's not a joke. It's a nothing. It's empty.*

With writing stories, I can clothe myself in the characters and the landscape. The threads that make me, the secrets within me, they might be there, but if they are then they're in disguise. It's make-believe, they say. You think it's not real, but it's just undercover.

Here, there is no hiding. I am forced to tell truths; if we are to help anyone we must tell the truth, at least from time to time. We must pull the shadows back. We must be unafraid.

How Not to Kill Yourself. The title saved me. The title made it easier.

I found a comment on my website a whole month after it had been written (thanks website for keeping me on the ball), left by someone called Joe Biel representing Microcosm Publishing, interested in publishing my short nonfiction piece *How Not to Kill Yourself* as a physical zine.

Of course, it was spam.

Oddly specific spam, however. Hmm. I guessed it had to be a scam, instead. I mean, *HNTKY* had been the only thing I'd written that I hadn't done my utmost to send to everyone whose name began with a letter of the alphabet. I'd sent it to nobody, in fact. I'd forgotten I'd even written it. It was my only piece of nonfiction, too. Who'd be interested in that? Out of everything I'd ever written, this was the very last thing that should have been picked up. How did this Joe Biel find it? I was under the impression nobody was aware that I or anything I wrote even existed.

Still, worth a reply. You know, to make sure. No skin off my back.

So I emailed him. And I received a quick reply, which further surprised me by not asking for my bank details. And a back-and-forth began. I queried how he found me, and Joe said I'd been recommended to him by one Dr. Faith Harper from San Antonio, Texas. Who on earth was this Texan doctor? How did she find *HNTKY*? This still made no sense!

I looked up this Microcosm Publishing, as well as this Dr. Faith Harper, who I also emailed (and who turned out to be awesome), and I slowly came around to the idea that it was all genuine, and someone Proper was actually interested in publishing something I'd written (even if it was little and nonfiction).

I signed a small contract with Microcosm, and I told people about it, grudgingly. I delayed telling my parents until I next saw them in person. Not to make it a big surprise, but rather to downplay it. My girlfriend was all proud and stuff.

But it wasn't a Big Deal. It was a Tiny Deal. It had to be. It seemed to me that people were so pleased for me because I'd never really given them anything to be proud of before, at least not for a long, long time. I felt that keenly. But I was determined to manage my expectations. I'm a cynic and a pessimist, and I believe that it's better to expect nothing, or the worst, and be pleasantly surprised, than to expect the best and be continually crushed. Of course, I can't always keep to this—I still hope (I'd be long gone if I didn't), and I certainly have hoped each time I've written a book or short story that something would come of it. But nothing ever does and I'm still thin-skinned every time it happens. So, the more I can let go, the better.

Then Microcosm tells me it's been doing well (Why? Who's reading it? How are people hearing about it? This still makes no sense!) and that they want to make it into a paperback and maybe get it into bookshops.

Okay, so the Tiny Deal is now, officially, a Small Deal.

I'm very pleased, and incredibly thankful to Faith Harper and the whole Microcosm team for making it happen. But shush, don't spoil it. Don't jinx it. A Middle-Sized Deal might be just around the corner.

S.S.

A LIST OF THINGS TO GOOGLE

HELP & SUPPORT

"samaritans"

"psychology today promoting hope preventing suicide"

"time to change suicide suicidal thoughts"

"time to change depression personal blogs"

"matt haig reasons to stay alive"

"blue light blue depression posts"

WEBCOMICS & ART

"hyperbole and a half depression" (make sure you read both Adventures in Depression and Depression Part Two, which is even better)

"depression comix"

"optipress suicide"

"ruby etc tumblr"

"vague notions tumblr"

"abstract peaces tumblr"

OTHER

"superbetter game"

"gambit depression game"

"what's on your mind? youtube depression higtonbros"

"she's novel writing when you are depressed"

"creative something the link between depression and creativity"

"art history famous artists committed suicide"

"nihilist memes facebook"

And, of course:

"microcosm publishing"

ABOUT THE AUTHOR

Set Sytes was born in the misty, Arthurian woods of England and was raised by bears. He grew up learning how to do and be many things at the same time, including slaying monsters, rescuing damsels in distress (who turned out to be neither in distress nor, in fact, damsels), and commanding great armies (the strategy involved inevitably being "everybody charge at the enemy").

As the Real World struck with a calamitous clang, Set was found wandering around in the desolate aftermath, completely uncertain about what was now expected of him. He faffed and stumbled around for an embarassingly long time (sometimes failing quite spectacularly) and then finally turned his hand to the only thing he remembered being any good at as a kid: writing. He was relieved to break the curse of never having finished anything in his life, when he finished his first novel. Which was okay-ish.

Set has since authored many stories of darkness and weirdness and flights of fancy, including the sci-fi/fantasy/western novel **WULF**, the YA pirate fantasy **India Bones and the Ship of the Dead**, the thoroughly twisted dystopian thriller **Moral Zero**, and the fantasy/horror short story collections of **Faces in the Dark** and **Born to be Weird**.

Set requests politely that you don't put onions anywhere near his food.